A SKULL IN CONNEMARA

Martin McDonagh

The Royal Court Writers Series published by
Methuen Drama in association with
the Royal Court Theatre

The Royal Court Writers Aeries

Copyright © 1997 by Martin McDonagh
The right of Martin McDonagh to be identified as the author of this
work has been asserted by him in accordance with the Copyright, Designs
and Patents Act, 1988

2 4 6 8 10 9 7 5 3

First published in Great Britain in 1997 by Methuen Drama
Methuen Publishing Ltd
215 Vauxhall Bridge Road
London SW1V 1EJ

in association with the Royal Court Theatre

Methuen Publishing Ltd Reg No. 3543167

ISBN 0 413 71970 7

Typeset by Deltatype Ltd, Birkenhead, Merseyside
Printed and bound in Great Britain
by Cox & Wyman Ltd, Reading, Berkshire

Caution

The Royal Court Theatre &
Druid Theatre Company present

A Skull in Connemara

by Martin McDonagh

A Royal Court and Druid Theatre Company co-production.

*First performance as part of **The Leenane Trilogy** at the Town Hall Theatre, Galway. 3 June 1997.*

*First performance as part of **The Leenane Trilogy** at the Royal Court Theatre Downstairs, St Martin's Lane. 17 July 1997.*

The Royal Court Theatre is financially assisted by the Royal Borough of Kensington and Chelsea. Recipient of a grant from the Theatre Restoration Fund & from the Foundation for Sport & the Arts. The Royal Court's Play Development Programme is funded by the Audrey Skirball-Kenis Theatre. Supported by the National Lottery through the Arts Council of England. Royal Court Registered Charity number 231242.

How the Royal Court is brought to you

The Royal Court (English Stage Company Ltd) is supported financially by a wide range of public bodies and private companies, as well as its own trading activities. The company receives its principal funding from the **Arts Council of England**, which has supported the Royal Court since 1956. The **Royal Borough of Kensington & Chelsea** gives an annual grant to the Royal Court Young People's Theatre. The **London Boroughs Grants Committee** contributes to the cost of productions in the Theatre Upstairs.

Other parts of the company's activities are made possible by business sponsorships. Several of these sponsors have made a long-term commitment. 1996 saw the sixth Barclays New Stages Festival of Independent Theatre, supported throughout by **Barclays Bank**. **British Gas North Thames** supported three years of the Royal Court's Education Programme. Sponsorship by **WH Smith** helped to make the launch of the Friends of the Royal Court scheme so successful.

1993 saw the start of our association with the **Audrey Skirball-Kenis Theatre** of Los Angeles, which is funding a Playwrights Programme at the Royal Court. Exchange visits for writers between Britain and the USA complement the greatly increased programme of readings and workshops which have fortified the company's capability to develop new plays.

In 1988 the **Olivier Building Appeal** was launched, to raise funds to begin the task of restoring, repairing and improving the Royal Court Theatre, Sloane Square. This was made possible by a large number of generous supporters and significant contributions from the **Theatres Restoration Fund**, the **Rayne Foundation**, the **Foundation for Sport and the Arts** and the **Arts Council's Incentive Funding Scheme**.

The Company earns the rest of the money it needs to operate from the Box Office, from other trading and from transfers to the West End of plays such as **Death and the Maiden**, **Six Degrees of Separation**, **Oleanna** and **My Night With Reg**. But without public subsidy it would close immediately and its unique place in British theatre would be lost.

Every Friendship is give and take

You give us £20 each year and a one-off initial joining fee of £25 and we give you:

*Two top price tickets for every production in the Theatre Downstairs for only £5 each

*Two top price tickets for every production in the Theatre Upstairs for only £5 each

*Priority booking for all productions at the Royal Court

*Free tickets to selected Royal Court readings and other special events

*You will also receive a newsletter including articles from writers, directors and other artists working at the Royal Court, and special offers for other theatres and arts events

AFTER JOINING YOU WILL ONLY HAVE TO PURCHASE TWO TICKETS IN THE THEATRE DOWNSTAIRS AND YOU WILL HAVE ALREADY SAVED £9

TO JOIN SIMPLY COMPLETE THE FORM AVAILABLE AT THE BOX OFFICE COUNTER

The Royal Court has a track record of success; I am associated with it because it is uniquely placed to take advantage of the current climate of optimism, energy and innovation.

Our plans for the transformed theatre in Sloane Square include the latest stage technology, a cafe bar and improved audience facilities enabling us to anticipate the latest in contemporary drama whilst at the same time the refurbished building will bear testimony to our past successes.

I invite you to become part of these exciting plans.

Gerry Robinson
Chairman, Granada Group

If you would like more information please contact me at the Royal Court Theatre, St Martin's Lane, London WC2N 4BG.

The Royal Court Theatre, Sloane Square, was built in 1888 and is the longest-established theatre in England with the dedicated aim of producing new plays. We were thrilled to be awarded £16.2 million in

September 1995 - from the National Lottery through the Arts Council of England - towards the renovation and restoration of our 100-year old home. This award has provided us with a once-in-a-lifetime opportunity to bring our beautiful and important theatre up to date and redevelopment work is now in progress at our Sloane Square site.

However we have no wish for change for change's sake, and the key to our success will be continuity. The Royal Court's auditorium, for instance, has been an important factor in the success of the English Stage Company over 40 years. Nothing must be done to jeopardise that supportive relationship. Similarly, the recently improved facade is a much-loved and familiar face on Sloane Square. This will scarcely change. But everything else must and will, not simply because the structure is crumbling and the mechanical and electrical services outdated. The Royal Court building must evolve and change to both maintain its present well-earned position in British theatre and also to lead the way into the next century.

Building work in Sloane Square is now well underway, but one major problem remains: the Court must raise more than £5 million itself in order to complete the work. The rules of our Lottery award are clear: the Lottery will pay up to three quarters of the costs of the capital project but we must find over £5 million ourselves as Partnership Funding. To help reach our target, we have launched our *Stage Hands Appeal* which aims to raise over £500,000 towards this £5 million target from friends, audience members and the general public by the end of 1998. So far the appeal has met with great success, but the fact remains that we still have some way to go to reach our goal.

If you would like to help, please complete the donation form enclosed in this playtext (additional donation forms available from the Box Office) and return it to: Development Office, Royal Court Theatre Downstairs, St. Martin's Lane, London WC2N 4BG. For more information on our redeveloment project please call 0171 930 4253. For details on forthcoming productions in our temporary homes (at the Duke of York's and Ambassador's Theatres) contact the Box Office on 0171 565 5000.

You have one week to live.

The English Stage Company at the Royal Court Theatre

The English Stage Company was formed to bring serious writing back to the stage. The first Artistic Director, George Devine, wanted to create a vital and popular theatre. He encouraged new writing that explored subjects drawn from contemporary life as well as pursuing European plays and forgotten classics. When John Osborne's **Look Back in Anger** was first produced in 1956, it forced British Theatre into the modern age. In addition to plays by "angry young men", the international repertoire ranged from Brecht to Ionesco, Jean-Paul Sartre, Marguerite Duras, Wedekind and Beckett.

The ambition was to discover new work which was challenging, innovative and also of the highest quality, underpinned by the desire to discover a contemporary style of presentation. Early Court writers included Arnold Wesker, John Arden, David Storey, Ann Jellicoe, N F Simpson and Edward Bond. They were followed by David Hare and Howard Brenton, Caryl Churchill, Timberlake Wertenbaker, Robert Holman and Jim Cartwright. Many of their plays are now regarded as modern classics.

Many established playwrights had their early plays produced in the Theatre Upstairs including Anne Devlin, Andrea Dunbar, Sarah Daniels, Jim Cartwright, Clare McIntyre, Winsome Pinnock, Martin Crimp and Phyllis Nagy. Since 1994 there has been a major season of plays by writers new to the Royal Court, many of them first plays, produced in association with the *Royal National Theatre Studio* with sponsorship from *The Jerwood Foundation*. The writers included Joe Penhall, Nick Grosso, Judy Upton, Sarah Kane, Michael Wynne, Judith Johnson, James Stock, Simon Block and Mark Ravenhill. In 1996-97 The Jerwood Foundation sponsored the Jerwood New Playwrights season, a series of six plays by Jez Butterworth and Martin McDonagh and Ayub Khan-Din (in the Theatre Downstairs), Mark Ravenhill, Tamantha Hammerschlag and Jess Walters (in the Theatre Upstairs).

Theatre Upstairs productions have regularly transferred to the Theatre Downstairs, as with Ariel Dorfman's **Death and the Maiden**, Sebastian Barry's **The Steward of Christendom**, a co-production with *Out of Joint*, and Martin McDonagh's **The Beauty Queen Of Leenane,** a co-production with Druid Theatre Company. Some Theatre Upstairs productions have transferred to the West End, such as Kevin Elyot's **My Night With Reg** at the Criterion

and Mark Ravenhill's **Shopping and F£££ing** (a co-production with *Out of Joint)* at the Gielgud.

1992-1997 have been record-breaking years at the box-office with capacity houses for productions of **Faith Healer**, **Death and the Maiden**, **Six Degrees of Separation**, **King Lear**, **Oleanna**, **Hysteria**, **Cavalcaders**, **The Kitchen**, **The Queen & I**, **The Libertine**, **Simpatico**, **Mojo** and **The Steward of Christendom**.

Death and the Maiden and **Six Degrees of Separation** won the Olivier Award for Best Play in 1992 and 1993 respectively. **Hysteria** won the 1994 Olivier Award for Best Comedy, and also the Writers' Guild Award for Best West End Play. **My Night with Reg** won the 1994 Writers' Guild Award for Best Fringe Play, the Evening Standard Award for Best Comedy, and the 1994 Olivier Award for Best Comedy. Jonathan Harvey won the 1994 Evening Standard Drama Award for Most Promising Playwright, for **Babies**. Sebastian Barry won the 1995 Writers' Guild Award for Best Fringe Play for **The Steward of Christendom** and also the 1995 Lloyds Private Banking Playwright of the Year Award. Jez Butterworth won the 1995 George Devine Award for Most Promising Playwright, the 1995 Writers' Guild New Writer of the Year, the Evening Standard Award for Most Promising Newcomer and the 1995 Olivier Award for Best Comedy for **Mojo**. Phyllis Nagy won the 1995 Writers' Guild Award for Best Regional Play for **Disappeared**. Martin McDonagh won the 1996 George Devine Award for Most Promising Playwright, the 1996 Writers' Guild Best Fringe Play Award, and the 1996 Evening Standard Drama Award for Most Promising Newcomer for **The Beauty Queen of Leenane**. The Royal Court won the 1995 Prudential Award for the Theatre, and was the overall winner of the 1995 Prudential Award for the Arts for creativity, excellence, innovation and accessibility. The Royal Court won the 1995 Peter Brook Empty Space Award for innovation and excellence in theatre.

Now in its temporary homes The Duke Of York's and Ambassadors Theatres, during the two-year refurbishment of its Sloane Square theatre, the Royal Court continues to present the best in new work. After four decades the company's aims remain consistent with those established by George Devine. The Royal Court is still a major focus in the country for the production of new work. Scores of plays first seen at the Royal Court are now part of the national and international dramatic repertoire.

Druid Theatre Company

Druid Theatre Company was founded in 1975 by Garry Hynes, Mick Lally and Marie Mullen. Based in Galway, a growing city on the west coast of Ireland, and working from a theatre that seated 47 people, within a few years the company had evolved an ambitious repertoire and a dynamic style of the utmost professionalism.

The fact that Druid worked outside the theatrical mainstream (for many years it was the only professional theatre company in Ireland outside Dublin), allied with the pressure of the individual talents of its members, forced the company into a highly individual approach to all aspects of theatre. A distinctive style began to emerge particulary in the work of the company's leading actors including Marie Mullen, Sean McGinley, Maelíosa Stafford and Ray McBride and the work of artistic director Garry Hynes.

In 1983 the company began an association with one of Ireland's leading writers, Tom Murphy, and productions included **Conversations on a Homecoming,** and **Bailegangaire** with Siobhan McKenna. Both these productions were seen in London at the Donmar Warehouse along with Druid's acclaimed production of **The Playboy of the Western World**. In the late eighties the company toured internationally with visits to New York and Sydney as well as regular UK dates including Glasgow and London.

In 1990 Garry Hynes left the company to become Artistic Director of the Abbey Theatre and Maelíosa Stafford was appointed to succeed her. Under Mr Stafford's direction the company began a policy of nurturing young writers and successes included Vincent Woods' **At the Black Pig's Dyke** and **Song of the Yellow Bittern. At The Black Pig's Dyke** was seen in London and Toronto in 1993/94 and was the centrepiece of the Sydney Festival in January 1995.

In October 1994 Garry Hynes returned as Artistic Director and began developing a comprehensive programme of new work. **The Beauty Queen of Leenane** opened the Town Hall Theatre, Galway on 1 February 1996 and marked the stage debut of Martin McDonagh. Other writers under comission to Druid include Billy Roche, Marina Carr, Niall Williams and Frank McGuinness.

In late 1996 as well as playing the Royal Court Theatre Downstairs, **The Beauty Queen of Leenane** toured some of the most westerly communities in Europe including seven islands ranging from Oileán Chléire in West Cork to Rathlin Island in Antrim. 1996 also saw Druid celebrate its 21st birthday with a production of Brian Friel's **The Loves of Cass Maguire.**

In 1998 Druid will produce all of Synge's plays in repertoire under the title **A Story Told Forever.** This project will premiere on Inis Meáin in late May 1998 marking the centenary of the playwright's first visit the the island.

For Druid Theatre Company

Artistic Director **Garry Hynes**
General Manager **Louise Donlon**
Production Manager **Maurice Power**
Administrator **Maria Fleming**
Executive Assistant **Eoin Brady**
Casting **Maureen Hughes**

Druid Theatre Company
Druid Lane
Galway
Ireland
Telephone Box Office:
00 353 91 568617
Administration: 00 353 91 568660
Fax: 00 353 91 563109
email: druid@iol.ie

The Cripple of Inishmaan

a new play by Martin McDonagh

Auntie Eileen &
Auntie Kate

Cripple Billy

Mammy

Slippy Helen

Bartley

Johnnypateenmike

Photos: Gautier Deblonde

NT Royal National Theatre

In repertoire in the Lyttelton until 19 August

Box Office 0171-928 2252
First Call 0171-420 0000

Reg'd Charity

A Skull in Connemara

by Martin McDonagh

Cast

Mick Dowd	Mick Lally
Mary Rafferty	Anna Manahan
Martin Hanlon	David Wilmot
Tom Hanlon	Brían F. O'Byrne

Director	Garry Hynes
Designer	Francis O'Connor
Lighting Designer	Ben Ormerod
Sound Design	Bell Helicopter
Music	Paddy Cunneen
Production Managers	Ed Wilson (RCT)
	Maurice Power (Druid)
Assistant Production Manager	Mark Townsend (RCT)
Design/Construction Consultant	James Probert
Company Stage Manager	Maris Sharp (RCT)
Company Stage Manager	Mairéad McGrath (Druid)
Deputy Stage Manager	Sophie Gabszewicz
Druid 'Handover' Stage Management Team	Bernie Walsh & Niall Cranney
Costume Supervisor	Orfhlaith Stafford
Production Photographs	Ivan Kyncl
Set Construction	Stage Surgeons Ltd, PL Parsons Ltd, Scott Fleary Ltd.
Scenic Artist	Paddy Hamilton
Special Effects/Prop Makers	Mac Teo, Paula Conroy, Aquality

Special thanks to: Martin Riley, Lizz Poulter, Alan Clarke, the Town Hall Theatre, Galway and Druid Theatre Company production team.

The Royal Court would like to thank the following for their help with this production: Auditorium redesign by Ultz; auditorium ceiling constructed by Stage Surgeons Ltd (0171 237 2765), rigged and suspended by Vertigo Rigging Ltd; Wardrobe care by Persil and Comfort courtesy of Lever Brothers Ltd, refrigerators by Electrolux and Philips Major Appliances Ltd.; kettles for rehearsals by Morphy Richards; video for casting purposes by Hitachi; backstage coffee machine by West 9; furniture by Knoll International; freezer for backstage use supplied by Zanussi Ltd 'Now that's a good idea.' Hair styling by Carole at Moreno, 2 Holbein Place, Sloane Square 0171-730-0211; Closed circuit TV cameras and monitors by Mitsubishi UK Ltd. Natural spring water from Aqua Cool, 12 Waterside Way, London SW17 0XH, tel. 0181-947 5666. Overhead projector from W.H. Smith; Sanyo U.K for the backstage microwave.

Martin McDonagh (writer)

For the Royal Court: The Beauty Queen of Leenane (co-production with Druid).

Other theatre includes: The Banshees of Inisheer, The Lieutenant of Inishmore, The Maamturk Rifleman.

Paddy Cunneen (music)

For the Royal Court: The Leenane Trilogy (co-production with Druid), Portia Coughlan (& Abbey), The Treatment.

He is an Associate Director of Cheek By Jowl Theatre Company and has written music for all but one of the company's productions since 1988.

Other composition for theatre includes: Angels in America - parts 1 & 2; Peer Gynt, Fuente Ovejuna, The Birthday Party, The Recruiting Officer, Fair Ladies at Poem Cards, The Cripple of Inishmaan, The Sea, The Devil's Disciple, Blue Remembered Hills, Chips With Everything, Othello (RNT); The Alchemist, The Changeling, Richard III, The Painter of Dishonour (RSC); A Doll's House, Seagull (Abbey & Gate); Popcorn (Nottingham Playhouse).

As musical director: Sweeney Todd, A Little Night Music (RNT); Company - winner of Music Industry Award, Cabaret (Donmar Warehouse).

Composition for radio includes: Cymbeline, The Jew of Malta, Mr Wroe's Virgins, Burdalane, Henry IV - parts 1 & 2, Tamburlaine.

Film and television includes: The Pan Loaf, The Maitlands, Two Oranges and a Mango, You Drive Me, The Big Fish, Memory Man, Bite.

Bell Helicopter (sound design)

For the Royal Court: The Leenane Trilogy (co-production with Druid); The Lights Are on But Nobody's At Home.

Original music and sound designs include - For theatre/dance: Mrs Sweeney, Hit and Run (Mint Theatre); Independent State (Cremorne Theatre Brisbane, The Playhouse, Sydney Opera House); Revelations (Traverse, Waterman's Arts Centre); Urban Originals (Berlin New Music Festival); Departure Lounge (ICA). For film: Irene is Not Herself Anymore, Les Vampires, You Don't Say, Chocolate Acrobat, Mumford Diaries, Cities of Brick. For radio: Radio Works (Radio Granuille, Marseilles).

Installations include: Lines of Thought (Project Arts / La Friche); Statue and Other Moving Things (Project Arts Centre); Evening Echoes (Tour); The Width, Thickness and Viscosity of Ghosts (Spitalfields' Public Toilets); Absence (Whitechapel Art Gallery); Walking (Nose Paint, London); Eye Witness (Endeavor House).

Garry Hynes (director)

Founded Druid Theatre Company in 1975. Artistic Director 1975-1991 and again from 1995 to date. Artistic Director of the Abbey Theatre, Dublin 1991-1994.

For the Royal Court: Portia Coughlan (& Abbey), A Whistle in the Dark (& Abbey); The Beauty Queen of Leenane (co-produced with Druid).

Other theatre includes: The Loves of Cass MacGuire, The Playboy of the Western World, Bailegangaire, Conversations on a Homecoming, Wood of the Whispering, 'Tis A Pity She's A Whore, Poor Beast in the Rain (Druid); King of the Castle, The Plough and the Stars, The Power of Darkness, Famine (Abbey); The Man of Mode, Song of the Nightingale (RSC); The Colleen Bawn (Royal Exchange Manchester). She is an Associate Director at the Royal Court.

Mick Lally

A founder member of Druid Theatre Company in 1975.

Theatre includes: The Loves of Cass Maguire, Wild Harvest, A Touch of the Poet, A Whistle in the Dark, Waiting for Godot, The Playboy of the Western World, The Glass Menagerie, Who's Afraid of Virginia Woolf? (Druid); Dectire, Studs (Passion Machine); Winter Thief (Peacock); The Honey Spike, A Crucial Week in the Life of a Grocer's Assistant, Drama at Inish, The Power of Darkness (Abbey); The Man From Clare, Moll, The Year of the Hiker (Gaiety); Fathers and Sons (Gate); Translations (Field Day).

Film and television includes: The Secret of Roan Inish, A Man of No Importance, Circle of Friends, Glenroe, Bracken, Roma, Tales of Kinvarna, Year of the French.

Anna Manahan

For the Royal Court: Live Like Pigs, The Beauty Queen of Leenane (co-production with Druid).

Other theatre includes: The Loves of Cass

Maguire, I Do Not Like Thee, Dr Fell (Druid);
Lovers (London and USA, nomination Tony
Award); The Shaughraun (Abbey); The
Matchmaker, The Streets of Dublin (Tivoli);
The Tailor and Ansty (Andrews Lane, Tivoli);
The Guernica Hotel, Happy Birthday Dear
Alice, The Crucible, The Old Lady's Guide to
Survival (Red Kettle).
Anna worked extensively with the Edwards
MacLiammoir Company, The Gate Theatre
and all the major Irish companies, as well as
Phyllis Ryan and Gemini Productions and
the Royal National Theatre.
Film and television includes: The Bill, Lovejoy,
The Young Indiana Jones Chronicles, The
Treaty, Blind Justice, A Man of No Importance,
Hear My Song, The Irish RM, Me Mammy.

Brían F. O'Byrne
For the Royal Court: The Beauty Queen of
Leenane (co-production with Druid).
Other theatre includes: Good Evening Mr
Collins (Peacock); Sharon's Grave (Gate);
The Drum (Co-Motion); Hapgood (Lincoln
Centre, New York); The Sisters Rosensweig
Barrymore, New York); Marking (Pure Or-
ange, New York); Seconds Out (Public, New
York); The Madam Macadam Travelling
Theatre Company, Grandchild of Kings (The
Irish Repertory Theatre Company, New York);
Philadelphia Here I Come, The Playboy of
the Western World, The Drum, Angel (Pedal
Crank, New York); A Thousand Hours of
Love (Theatre for New City, New York); The
Country Boy, Moll (Irish Theatre Company,
Buffalo).
Film includes: The Last Bus Home, The Fifth
Province, Avenue X.

Francis O'Connor (designer)
For the Royal Court: The Beauty Queen of
Leenane (co-production with Druid).
Other design for theatre includes: Wild
Harvest (Druid); Tarry Flynn, The Importance
of Being Earnest, She Stoops to Folly,
Silverlands (Abbey); The Bread Man (Gate);
All in the Timing, Aladdin, Dick Whittington
(Nottingham Playhouse); The Clearing
(Bush); After Easter (RSC); Sing to the Dawn,
Little Shop of Horrors, Into the Woods
(Singapore); Moby Dick (Germany); The Ugly
Duckling (Watermill); Annie (Crucible).
Design for opera includes: Ariadne Auf Naxos
(Castleward); Linda Di Chamounix
(Guildhall); May Night (Wexford Festival); La

Vie Parisienne (D'Oyly Carte); The Barber of
Seville (English Touring Opera); Rape of
Lucretia (Guildhall); Pirates of Penzance
(Cleveland Theatre Company); La Boheme
(Stowe Opera).
Future projects include: Enter the Guardsman
(Donmar Warehouse); Love on the Throne
(Nottingham Playhouse).

Ben Ormerod (lighting designer)
For the Royal Court: The Beauty Queen of
Leenane (co-production with Druid).
Other lighting design for theatre includes:
Uncle Vanya, Accidental Death of an
Anarchist, Bent, The Winter's Tale (RNT);
Hamlet, Twelfth Night, Comic Mysteries
(Oxford Stage Company); Hedda Gabler,
Hamlet (English Touring Theatre, Donmar
Warehouse); Oedipus Rex (Epidaurus);
Passing Places (Traverse); The House of
Bernarda Alba (Theatre Clwyd).
Lighting design for opera includes: Il
Trovatore (Scottish Opera); The Mask of
Orpheus (Royal Festival Hall); The Cunning
Peasant (Guildhall); Baa Baa Black Sheep
(Opera North & BBC2).
Future productions include; All's Well That
Ends Well (Oxford Stage Company); The
Seagull (English Touring Theatre, Donmar
Warehouse); A Time and a Season (Theatre
Royal, Plymouth).

David Wilmot
Theatre includes: Belfry, At the Black Pig's
Dyke (Druid); Six Characters in Search of an
Author, Rosencrantz and Guildernstern Are
Dead, Child's Christmas In Wales, King of
the Castle (Abbey); The Invisible Mending
Co (Peacock); The Plough and the Stars,
Juno and the Peacock (Rainbow, Carnival
Productions); The Risen People (Gaiety);
The Grogan Budgies (Project Theatre);
Murder in the Cathedral (Christchurch
Cathedral).
Film and television includes: The Last Bus
Home, I Went Down, The Devil's Own,
Michael Collins, The Field, Island of
Strangers, McCadden, The Bill, The Treaty,
Lapsed Catholics.

For the Royal Court

DIRECTION
Artistic Director
Stephen Daldry
Assistant to the
Artistic Director
Marieke Spencer
Deputy Director
James Macdonald
Associate Directors
Elyse Dodgson
Ian Rickson
Garry Hynes*
Max Stafford-Clark*
Caroline Hall*
Roxana Silbert*
Stephen Warbeck (music)*
Trainee Director
Rufus Norris #
Casting Director
Lisa Makin
Literary Manager
Graham Whybrow
Literary Assistant
Jean O'Hare
Literary Associate
Stephen Jeffreys*
Resident Dramatist
Martin Crimp+
International Assistant
Aurélie Mérel
Artistic Assistant
Rachael Prior

PRODUCTION
Production Manager
Edwyn Wilson
Deputy Production
Manager
Paul Handley
Production Development
Manager
Simon Harper
Head of Lighting
Johanna Town
Senior Electricians
Alison Buchanan
Lizz Poulter
Assistant Electricians
Marion Mahon
Lars Jensen
LX Board Operator
Michelle Green
Head of Stage
Martin Riley
Senior Carpenters
David Skelly
Christopher Shepherd
Terry Bennett
Head of Sound
Paul Arditti
Deputy Sound
Simon King
Sound Assistant
Neil Alexander
Production Assitant
Mark Townsend
Head of Wardrobe
Jennifer Cook
Costume Deputies
Neil Gillies
Heather Tomlinson

MANAGEMENT
Executive Director
Vikki Heywood
Assistant to the
Executive Director
Diana Pao
Administrator
Alpha Hopkins
Finance Director
Donna Munday
Finance Officer
Rachel Harrison
Re-development
Finance Officer
Neville Ayres
Project Manager
Tony Hudson
Assistant to
Project Manager
Monica McCormack
Finance & Administration
Assistant
Sarah Deacon

MARKETING & PRESS
Marketing Manager
Jess Cleverly
Press Manager
Anne Mayer (0171-565 5055)
Marketing Co-ordinator
Lisa Popham
Publicity Assistant
Peter Collins
Box Office Manager
Neil Grutchfield
Deputy Box Office Manager
Terry Cooke
Box Office Sales Operators
Glen Bowman
Valli Dakshinamurthi
Ian Golding
Emma O'Neill
Ruth Goucheron*
Azieb Zerai*

DEVELOPMENT
Development Director
Caroline Underwood
Head of Development
Joyce Hytner
Development Manager
Jacqueline Simons
Development Co-ordinator
Susie Songhurst*
Development Assistant
Tracey Nowell

FRONT OF HOUSE
Theatre Manager
Gary Stewart
Deputy Theatre Managers
Yvette Griffith
Tim Brunsden
Duty House Manager
Rachel Fisher*
Relief Duty House Managers
Sarah Harrison*
Anthony Corriette*
Lorraine Selby*
Jemma Davies*
Bookshop Supervisor
Del Campbell*
Maintenance
Greg Piggot*
Lunch Bar Caterer
Andrew Forrest*
Stage Door/Reception
Jemma Davies*

Lorraine Benloss*
Charlotte Frings*
Tyrone Lucas*
Andonis Anthony*
Tom Cockrell*
Cleaners
(Theatre Upstairs)
Maria Correia*
Mila Hamovic*
Peter Ramswell*
(Theatre Downstairs)
Avery Cleaning Services Ltd.
Fireman
Myriad Security Services
(Theatre Downstairs)
Datem Fire Safety Services
(Theatre Upstairs)
Thanks to all of our
bar staff and ushers

YOUNG PEOPLE'S THEATRE
Director
Carl Miller
Youth Drama Worker
Ollie Animashawun
Special Projects
Julie-Anne Robinson
Administrator
Aoife Mannix
Outreach Co-ordinator
Stephen Gilroy

ENGLISH STAGE COMPANY
President
Greville Poke
Vice President
Joan Plowright CBE

COUNCIL
Chairman
John Mortimer QC, CBE
Vice-Chairman
Anthony Burton

Stuart Burge
Harriet Cruickshank
Stephen Evans
Sonia Melchett
James Midgley
Richard Pulford
Gerry Robinson
Timberlake Wertenbaker
Nicholas Wright
Alan Yentob

ADVISORY COUNCIL
Diana Bliss
Tina Brown
Allan Davis
Elyse Dodgson
Robert Fox
Jocelyn Herbert
Michael Hoffman
Hanif Kureishi
Jane Rayne
Ruth Rogers
James L. Tanner

*=part-time
#=Arts Coucil of England/Calouste Gulbenkian
Foundation/Esmeé Fairbairn Charitable Trust
+ = Arts Council Resident Dramatist

A Skull in Connemara

Characters

Mick Dowd, *fifties*
Maryjohnny Rafferty, *seventies*
Mairtin Hanlon, *late teens / early twenties*
Thomas Hanlon, *thirties*

Setting
Rural Galway

Scene One

*The fairly spartan main room of a cottage in rural Galway. Front
door stage left, a table with two chairs and a cupboard towards the
right, and a lit fireplace in the centre of the back wall with an
armchair on each side of it. A crucifix hangs on the back wall and an
array of old farm tools, sickles, scythes and picks etc., hang just below
it. At the start of the play,* **Mick Dowd**, *a man in his fifties
whose cottage it is, is sitting in the left armchair as* **Mary
Rafferty**, *a heavy-set, white-haired neighbour in her seventies,
knocks and is let in through the front door.*

Mary   Mick.

Mick   Maryjohnny.

Mary   Cold.

Mick   I suppose it's cold.

Mary   Cold, aye. It's turning.

Mick   Is it turning?

Mary   It's turning now, Mick. The summer is going.

Mick   It isn't going yet, or is it now?

Mary   The summer is going, Mick.

Mick   What month are we now?

Mary   Are we September?

Mick (*thinks*)   We are, d'you know?

Mary   The summer is going.

Mick   What summer we had.

Mary   What summer we had. We had no summer.

Mick   Sit yourself down for yourself, there, Mary.

Mary (*sitting*)   Rain, rain, rain, rain, rain we had. And
now the cold. And now the dark closing in. The leaves'll be
turning in a couple of weeks, and that'll be the end of it.

Mick   I didn't even know it *was* September, and I'll admit it.

Mary   Did you not now, Mick? What month did you think it was?

Mick   August or something I thought it was.

Mary   August? (*Laughs.*) August is gone.

Mick   I know it is, now.

Mary   August went.

Mick   I know it did.

Mary   Last month August was.

Mick (*slightly irritated*)   I know it was now, Mary. You don't have to keep saying.

Mary (*pause*)   Didn't the boys and girls go back to school, and stopped parading up and down the street like . . .

Mick   Ah sure they did. And don't I usually notice that one, and say to meself, 'The boys and girls have gone back to school. The summer is surely over now.'

Mary   Like a pack o' whores.

Mick (*pause*)   Who's like a pack o' whores?

Mary   Them schoolies parading up and down.

Mick   I wouldn't say a pack o' whores, now.

Mary   Kissing.

Mick   What harm?

Mary   Cursing.

Mick   Mary, you're too old-fashioned, so you are. Who doesn't curse nowadays?

Mary   I don't.

Mick   'You don't.'

Mary (*pause*) Eamonn Andrews didn't.

Mick Well we can't all be as good as you or Eamonn Andrews. And I'll bet Eamonn Andrews would've cursed too were he to've fell, or sat on a nail.

Mary He would not.

Mick It's only on television you ever saw. When he got home he probably cursed a-plenty. He probably did nothing but curse.

Mary Oh, a lie now . . .

Mick When he got home now, I'm saying.

Mary I'll tell you someone else who doesn't curse. (*Pointing to the crucifix.*) That man doesn't curse.

Mick Well we can't all be as good as Our Lord. Let alone Eamonn Andrews. Now those youngsters are only out for a bit of fun during their holidays, and not meaning no harm to anybody.

Mary No harm to anybody, is it, Mick? And the three I caught weeing in the churchyard and when I told them I'd tell Father Cafferty, what did they call me? A fat oul biddy!

Mick I know they did, Mary, and they shouldn't've . . .

Mary I know well they shouldn't've!'

Mick That was twenty-seven years ago for God's sake, Mary.

Mary Twenty-seven years ago or not!

Mick You should let bygones be bygones.

Mary Bygones, is it? No, I will not let bygones be bygones. I'll tell you when I'll let bygones be bygones. When I see them burned in Hell I'll let bygones be bygones, and not before!

Mick Hell is too harsh a price just for weeing. Sure they were only five, God bless them.

Mary   On consecrated ground, Mick.

Mick   On consecrated ground or not. They may have
been bursting. And what's consecrated ground anyways but
any old ground with a dab of holy water pegged on it?

Mary   Well, you would be the man, Mick Dowd, I'd
expect would argue that, the filthy occupation you take on
every autumntime . . .

Mick (*interrupting*)   There's no need for that.

Mary   Is there no need for that, now?

Mick *gets up, pours out two glasses of poteen, gives one to* **Mary**
and sits down with the other.

Mick   Doesn't the County pay for the job to be done if
it's such a filthy occupation? Doesn't the priest half the
time stand over me and chat to me and bring me cups of
tea? Eh?

Mary (*pause*)   I suppose he does. (*Sips her poteen.*) Not that
I'd give a bent ha'penny for that young skitter.

Mick   What young skitter?

Mary   Father Welsh, Walsh, Welsh.

Mick   Nothing the matter with Father Welsh.

Mary   Nothing the matter at all, except I don't too much
like going to confession with a gasur aged two!

Mick   What the Hell sins do you have to confess to him
every week anyways?

Mary   What sins do *you* confess would be more in your
line.

Mick (*playfully*)   What would it be, now? It wouldn't be
impure thoughts? Ah no. It must be 'Thou shalt not steal'
so.

Mary   How, 'Thou shalt not steal'?

Mick   Oh, cadging off the Yanks a pound a throw the

maps the Tourist Board asked you to give them for free. Telling them your Liam's place was where *The Quiet Man* was filmed, when wasn't it a hundred miles away in Ma'am Cross or somewhere?

Mary A hundred miles is it? Ma'am Cross has moved so, because eight miles it was the last time I looked.

Mick John Wayne photos, two pound a pop. Maureen O'Hara drank out of this mug – a fiver. Boy, I'll tell you, anh? Them eejit Yanks.

Mary If the eejit Yanks want to contribute a couple of bob to an oul lady's retirement, I'll not be standing in their way, sure.

Mick So if it's not cadging off them thicks you confess it must be playing the ten books the bingo, so.

Mary (*smiling*) I don't play ten books the bingo.

Mick Oh, the County could round up a hundred witnesses would tell you the differ, 'cos twenty year it's been going on now.

Mary Maybe now and then I do forget how many books I've picked up . . .

Mick Forget, is it?

Mary (*slightly hurt*) It's forget, Mick. I do mean to pick up the four, and then two books get stuck together, and before I know where I am I'm sitting down and how many books do I have . . .

Mick Mary Rafferty, you have played ten books in that church hall for every week since de Valera was twelve, and it's ten books if they're lucky, because doesn't it rise to fifteen when the Christmas jackpot draws on, and isn't it twenty-two books at once your Guinness World's record is, and wouldn't it be higher still if it wasn't eighteen times you won that night and you thought they might begin to get suspicious?

Mary *stares at him angrily.*

Mary   Well on the subject of confession, now, Mick Dowd, how long is it since *you've* seen the priest? Seven and a half years, is it, Mick?

Mick   Eh?

Mary   Seven and a half . . .

Mick (*angrily*)   That's enough of that, now, Mary.

Mary   Wasn't it your Oona used to drag you there of a week . . . ?

Mick (*angrily, standing*)   That's enough of that now, I said! Or else be off with you!

He idles a little, pouring himself another drink.

Mary   He calls too slow anyways.

Mick   Who calls too slow?

Mary   That skitter at St Patrick's the bingo.

Mick   Oh, calls the bingo.

Mary   Walsh, Welsh. (*Pause.*) You need ten books to make it worthwhile, else you'd be hanging about, so. It isn't to win I have ten books.

Mick   It's the game of it.

Mary   It's the game of it, Mick, is right.

Mick   Nobody begrudges you anyways.

Mary   Because I'm oul.

Mick   Nobody begrudges you still.

A knock at the front door, which pushes open immediately. **Mairtin** *enters in a Man. Utd away shirt with 'Keane' on the back, blowing bubbles now and then.*

Mairtin   How is all?

Mary   How are you, Mairtin?

Mick   How are you, Mairtin? And close the door.

Mairtin   I'll close the door (*Does so.*) or was it a barn with a wide open door you were born in, me mam says. She says, was it a barn with a wide open door you were born in, Mary beag, and I say 'You're the get would know, Mam.'

Mary *tuts.*

Mairtin   No, I say, you're the woman would know, Mam. I do. That's what I say, like. Because if anybody was to know where I was born, wouldn't it be her? (*Pause.*) The Regional Hospital I was born. In Galway.

Mick   We know where the Regional Hospital is.

Mairtin   Aye. (*To* **Mary**.) Wasn't it you was in there with your hip?

Mary   No.

Mairtin   It must've been somebody else so. Aye. Who was it? Somebody who fell down and was fat.

Mick   What is it you've come over about, Mairtin?

Mairtin   Father Welsh or Walsh sent me over. It was choir and I was disruptive. Is that poteen, Mick? You wouldn't spare a drop?

Mick   No I wouldn't.

Mairtin   Ah g'wan . . .

Mary   Why was you being disruptive in choir, Mairtin? You used to be a good little singer, God bless you.

Mairtin   Ah, a pack of oul shite they sing now.

Mary *tuts at his language.*

Mairtin   A pack of not very good songs they sing now, I mean. All wailing, and about fishes, and bears.

Mick   About fishes and bears, is it?

Mairtin   It is. That's what *I* said, like. They said no, the youngsters like these ones. What's the song they had us

singing tonight? Something about if I was a bear I'd be
happy enough, but I'm even more glad I'm human. Ah, a
pile of oul wank it is. It's only really the Christmas carols I
do like.

Mick   And in September you don't get too much call for
them.

Mairtin   Is right, you don't. But I think they should have
them all year, instead of the skitter they do, because they
do make you very Christmassy, like.

Mary   How is mam and dad, Mairtin, I haven't seen
them a few days?

Mairtin   Oh, grand indeed, now. Or anyway me mam's
grand and me dad's as grand as a bastard of a get like him
can be . . .

Mary   Mairtin. Your own father now.

Mairtin   My own father is right. And if he took his belt
off to you for no reason at all eight times a week, it
wouldn't be so quick you'd be saying 'Your own father
now'. I'll tell you that.

Mick   And you don't do anything to deserve it, I
suppose? Ah no.

Mairtin   Not a thing.

Mick   Not a thing, oh aye. Not even the guards' tyres got
slashed outside the disco in Carraroe, your pal Ray Dooley
got nabbed for, someone else ran away.

Mairtin   Wasn't me now, Mick.

Mick   Oh no. Of course.

Mairtin   I had a bad leg anyways, and what were the
guards doing in the disco that time of night anyway is what
I'd like to know.

Mick   Routing out the yobbos who started the bottle fight
that the two wee girls got taken the night to hospital from.

Mairtin   Well you'd think they'd have something better to do with their time.

Mick   Uh-huh. What was Welsh's message, Mairtin?

Mairtin   And maybe them two girls deserved a bottling anyways. You don't know the full facts.

Mary   Why would poor girls deserve a bottling, sure?

Mairtin   Every why. Maybe the piss out of a fella's trainers they took, when all he did was ask them for a danceen, and polite. And then called their bastard brother over to come the hard. Stitches aren't good enough for them sorts of bitches, and well they know. As ugly as them two started out, sure stitches'd be nothing but an improvement, oh aye. (*Pause.*) But as I say, I wasn't there, now, I had a bad leg.

Mick   Are you going to make me ask me question again, Mairtin?

Mairtin   What question?

Mick   What was Welsh's fecking message, for Christ's sake?!

Mairtin (*pause*)   Shouting is it, Mick? You're to make a start on this year's exhuming business this coming week. The graveyard shenanigans.

Mary *looks across at* **Mick** *with stern resentment.* **Mick** *avoids her gaze somewhat guiltily.*

Mick   This coming week? That's early. In the year, I mean. Although with them burying poor Mag Folan last month there I suppose has hurried things along a little.

Mairtin   I don't know if it's hurried things along a little and I don't care if it's hurried things along a little. I'm to help you anyways and twenty quid the week oul Walsh, oul Welsh is to be giving me.

Mick   You're to help me?

Mairtin   Oul Welsh said. Aye. Twenty quid the week.

How much do you get the week, Mick?

Mick   I get enough the week, and what matter is it to you?

Mairtin   No matter at all, now. Only wondering, I was.

Mick   Well don't be wondering.

Mairtin   Sure, you're the experienced man, anyways. If it's a hundred or if it's more than a hundred, you deserve it, for you're the experienced man. (*Pause.*) Is it more than a hundred, Mick, now?

Mick   This ladeen.

Mairtin   Sure I'm only asking, sure.

Mick   Well that's what you do best is ask eejit questions.

Mairtin   Oh, eejit questions, is it?

Mick   It is.

Mairtin   Ah . . . ah . . . hmm.

Mary   It's more than you, Mairtin, has questions that that man will not answer.

Mick   Oh, now you're starting with your oul woman bull.

Mairtin   What kind of questions, Mary beag?

Mary   Questions about where did he put our Padraig when he dug him up is the kind of question, and where did he put our Bridgit when he dug her up is the kind of question, and where did he put my poor ma and da when he dug them up is the biggest question!

Mairtin   Where *did* you put all Mary's relations, Mick then, now? The oul bones and the whatnot.

Mary   He won't let on.

Mick   Will I not let on?

Mary   Let on so.

Mairtin   Aye, let on so.

Mick Oh, now you're chipping in.

Mairtin I *am* chipping in. What did you do with them?

Mick What did I do with them, is it?

Mairtin It is. For the hundredth fecking time it is.

Mick Oh, for the hundredth fecking time, is it? I'll tell you what I did with them. I hit them with a hammer until they were dust and I pegged them be the bucketload into the slurry.

Mary *is aghast.* **Mairtin** *bursts out laughing loudly.*

Mairtin *(laughing)* Is that true, now?

Mick Oh, maybe it's true now, and maybe it isn't at all.

Mairtin You hit them with a hammer and you pegged them in the slurry? Can I do that, now, Mick?

Mick No, you can't do that.

Mairtin Ah, you don't hammer no corpses at all. Probably seal them up and put them somewhere is all you do. Put them in the lake or somewhere, when no beggar's about.

Mick Maybe it's in the lake I put them, aye. This is the expert.

Mary *has been keeping* **Mick** *in a stern, fixed stare all the while.*

Mary Mick Dowd!

Mick Maryjohnny!

Mary I am going to ask you one question! And I want the truth!

Mick Ask away for yourself!

Mary Is that right what you said that you hammer the bones to nothing and you throw them in the slurry?

Mick What I do with the bones, both the priest and the guards have swore me to secrecy and bound by them I am . . .

Mairtin Oh ho.

Mary (*standing*) Michael Dowd, if you do not answer, bound or not bound, I shall leave this devil-taken house and never darken its . . . !

Mick Bound I am by the priest and the guards . . .

Mary Michael Dowd, if you do not answer . . .

Mick I neither hammer the bones nor throw them in the slurry, Mary. Sure what do you take me for?

Mairtin I knew well, sure . . .

Mary So what is it you do with them so, if it isn't hammer?

Mick (*pause*) I seal them in a bag and let them sink to the bottom of the lake and a string of prayers I say over them as I'm doing so.

Mairtin I told you, now, it was the fecking lake, or the lake rather. Didn't I tell you now that that's what it was, that he sealed them in a bag and he pegged them in the lake?

Mick I didn't say I pegged them. I said I gently *eased* them.

Mairtin Oh aye, you eased them in there, like. And said a couple of prayers over them, aye.

Mick And said a couple of prayers over them.

Mairtin To make it official, like.

Mary Is that the truth, Mick Dowd?

Mick That's the truth, Mary beag.

Mary I shall sit and finish that sup with you, so.

Mick Good on you, Mary.

Mary *sits back down.* **Mick** *refills her glass.*

Mairtin (*eyeing the poteen*) After seven years, sure, it's only a poor straggle of two or three bones they are anyway, I'm sure, and nothing to hammer at all.

Mick The expert on the matter now we're listening to.

Mairtin It's nothing to do with expert. Pure oul common sense is all it has to do with.

Mick Now you're explaining it to me.

Mairtin There's been a cow in our field dead four or five years . . .

Mick I know there has. And that's the best cow you have.

Mairtin No, no, now. Not the best cow we have. It wasn't even our cow at all. Didn't it just wander into our fields one day and fall over dead?

Mick Aye. The smell knocked it.

Mairtin And isn't it now just the . . . 'The smell knocked it.' Feck you. The smell of this house? Eh? 'The smell knocked it'? I'll tell you, boy, eh? (*Pause.*) What was it I was saying, now? You've made me forget . . .

Mick 'Isn't it now just the something . . .'

Mairtin Isn't it now just the skull and a couple of bones left on it, the cow, and no hide nor hair other than that? So wouldn't the body of a person be even less than that, it being rotting in the ground?

Mick You have a point there. Except the body of a person your family wouldn't have been picking at for ye're dinners the last five years.

Mairtin Picking at it for our dinners, is it? We do have a sight better dinners in our house than you do in this fecking house anyways! I'll tell you that now! Poteen breakfasts and poteen suppers is all I ever see consumed in this house!

Mick True enough for yourself.

Mairtin   Eh? Insulting our mam's dinners, when all it was was explaining about the cow in our field and the bones was all I was doing. Explaining, so as to help you.

Mick   You're right there, now, Mairtin. I wasn't thinking.

Mairtin   Right? I know I'm right.

Mick   And if I insulted you or your mam or your mam's dinners by casting aspersions you pick the meat off cows five years dead and can't tell the differ, then I take it all back and I apologise.

Mairtin (*confused*)   Eh? Uh-huh? Well, okay. Good.

Mick *pours himself another drink.*

Mairtin   And just to show there's no hard feelings, the tiniest of sips, now, let me take a taste of, Mick. This much, even.

Mick   That much, is it?

Mairtin   That's all. To show there's no hard feelings, now.

Mick   To show there's no hard feelings, aye.

He pours a small amount of poteen out onto his fingers and tosses it at **Mairtin** *as if it's holy water. It hits* **Mairtin** *in the eyes.*

Bless yourself, now, Mairtin.

Mary *laughs slightly.* **Mick** *sits back down.* **Mairtin** *rubs his eyes angrily.*

Mairtin   Got me in the eye, that did!

Mick   Sure that's where I was aiming. I'll bet it stung too.

Mairtin   It *did* sting too, you stinking fecker you. (**Mary** *tuts.*) Tut at me, you? Tut at him would be more in your line when he throws poteen in me eyes, near blinds me.

Mary   You'll know now not again to be disruptive in choir, Mairtin beag.

Mairtin   Choir?! What has fecking choir to do with

anything?! He insults me mam's cooking, throws poteen in me eyes.

Mick Sure it was only a drop, sure. Would I be wasting good poteen on your eyes?

Mairtin (*to* **Mary**) Has it gone red, Gran?

Mary A bit red, Mairtin . . .

Mick 'Gone red.' Jeez, you always was a wussy oul pussy, Mairtin, and nothing but a wussy oul pussy.

Mairtin A wussy oul pussy, is it?

Mick It is.

Mairtin Well maybe I am at that, and maybe I know something that you don't know too.

Mick What do you know? Skitter you know, Mairtin beag.

Mairtin Maybe I know which corner of the cemetery it is we're to be digging this week.

Mick What do I care which corner of the cemetery?

Mairtin Oh, maybe you don't, now. Only that it's the south side, by the gable.

Mick *nods, somewhat disturbed.*

Mick Are they all more than seven years down, then, at the gable. They are, I suppose.

Mairtin They are. Seven years and more! (*To* **Mary**.) See? He doesn't like it when it starts to get closer to home. That's when he doesn't like it.

Mary What do you mean, 'closer to home'?

Mairtin Isn't it his missus buried down there by the gable? How closer to home can you get?

Mary Is Oona buried at the gable, Mick, now?

Mick She is.

Mary   Oh, God love you . . .

Mairtin   That'll be an interesting job anyways. It isn't many's the man gets paid for digging up the bones of his own dead wife.

Mick   Oona left those bones a long time ago, and that's the only thing that they are now, is bones.

Mary (*quietly*)   You can't go digging up Oona, Mick. That's not right. Leave Oona to somebody else, now.

Mick   To who? To him? He'd probably crack her head in two, so he would.

Mairtin   Oh. Crack her head in two, is it?

Mick   It is.

Mairtin   I heard that's already been done.

Mick (*pause. Standing, advancing*)   What did you hear?

Mairtin   Just a thing or two, now, and don't you be fecking advancing on me, because saying nothing I was, only some people say things and I pay no mind at all until some other people start shouting the odds and calling me names and pegging poteen in me eyes . . .

Mick   What names did I call you?

Mary (*pause. Quietly*)   A wussy oul pussy . . .

Mairtin   A wussy oul pussy you called me. And if people start doing that then I'll have to be pegging something back at them, and it isn't a smatter of poteen it'll be, it'll be aspersions. And if the aspersions are true or not I don't know, and I don't care. I only threw them out because it was you who started the whole shebang in the first place.

Mick   What *are* the aspersions anyways?

Mairtin   Just general ones.

Mick   The only aspersions that could be cast are the ones I've already admitted to, and the ones I've already served me time over. That I had had a drink taken, and a good drink, and that she had no seat-belt on her, and that was the end of it. No other aspersions could there be.

Mairtin   Well, sure, that was the aspersion I was saying anyways, the drink-driving aspersion. What aspersion did you think I was saying?

Mick (*pause*)   That was the aspersion you was saying?

Mairtin   Aye. (*Pause.*) What was . . .

Mick   Well even that aspersion is seven years past, yet straight to me face you go casting your fecking . . .

Mairtin   Well isn't that better than the most of them round here? Will smile at you 'til you're a mile away before they start talking behind your back. One thing about me, anyways. I'm honest.

Mick (*to* **Mary**)   Do people be talking behind my bank?

Mary   They do not. He's a wee get with nothing but cheek.

Mairtin   A wee get is it? And they don't be talking behind his back? Uh-huh. It must be some other fella who drove his wife into a wall, so, they must be talking about. I must be mistaken. I often am.

Mick (*quietly*)   Leave this house, Mairtin Hanlon.

Mairtin   I *will* leave this house, the welcome I got here, after coming all this way with the message from oul Welsh, Walsh, Welsh. Not only no welcome but a spray of poteen that almost took me eyes out as a thank you, not to mention the names called, and the insulted mam's dinners. Uh-huh. (*At door.*) Um . . . will they have a spade at the church I can use, Mick, for I have no spade?

Mary   Your father has a rake of spades, sure.

Mairtin *examines the sharpness of some of the tools on the back wall.*

Mairtin   My father has no rake of spades. He has a rake of rakes. He has no spade. The only spade he has are the handles of two spades, and nothing but the handles, which you couldn't call a spade at all. Rakes he has a stack of, and I don't know why, because there is no call for them. There is always more call for a spade than a rake. In my opinion.

Mick   They'll have a spade at the church.

Mairtin   Will they have a spade at the church? Except they'll need two spades. One for the both of us . . .

Mick   They'll have two spades.

Mairtin   Are you positive, now? I don't want to be walking all that way . . .

Mick   Mairtin, will you ever feck off home for yourself?!

Mairtin   Feck off home, is it? I'll feck off home, all right. I don't have to be asked twice.

Mick   No, fecking five times you have to be asked!

Mairtin (*exiting*)   Uh-huh, I don't have to be asked twice.

Mary (*pause*)   The tongue on that one.

Pause. They drink their poteen a while, staring into the fire.

Mick   Is it true, Mary?

Mary   Is what true, Mick?

Mick   The talking behind my back.

Mary   There is no talking behind your back. He's a wee eejit, or if not an eejit then a blackguard, and we both know the truth of that.

Mick   Aye.

Mary   Sure the time he put the werewolf comic in with Mrs Dunphy, and hadn't they almost nailed the lid on her before we noticed?

Mick   Aye.

Mary   If that had gone ahead, just think. (*Pause.*) The boy's a wee blackguard and nothing else, and even though he's me own grandson I'll admit it, he's a rotten blackguard with nothing but cheek, so don't you even be thinking about it.

Mick   Aye. (*Pause.*) Aye, I suppose you're right.

Mary   I *am* right, sure.

Mick   Aye.

Mary   Right? There's no question, right.

Mick   There's not, I suppose. No. (*Pause.*) No. (*Pause.*) And there's been no other aspersions cast with my name on them, other than those . . .

Mary   There's been no other aspersions, Mick. (*Pause.*) None at all, sure. (*Pause.*) Sure we all know the type of man you are, Mick Dowd.

Mick *looks across at her.*

Mick   Aye . . . Is right.

Mary *smiles at him slightly. They both stare at the fire again. Curtain.*

Scene Two

A rocky cemetery at night, lit somewhat eerily by a few lamps dotted about. Two graves with gravestones atop a slight incline in the centre. At the start of the scene, the grave on the right is in the process of being dug up by **Mick**, *standing down inside it to waist height, shoveling the dirt out.* **Mairtin** *lays his shovel down, sits against the right-hand gravestone behind him, and lights a cigarette.*

Mairtin   I'm taking a cigarette break.

Mick   A break from what, sure? You've done no work.

Mairtin   I've done my biteen.

Mick   A bit of shite you've done.

Mairtin I have a blister too, and I didn't even mention it.

Mick You've mentioned it now.

Mairtin For fear I'd be accused of complaining. (*Pause. Looking at the next-door grave.*) When will we be starting on your missus's patch anyways? Going around in circles to avoid it we seem to be.

Mick We go in order. We don't skip two ahead.

Mairtin Skip? That's all we've been doing is skipping, if you're asking my opinion. (*Pause.*) *I'll* make a start on your missus's grave.

Mick Will you, now?

Mairtin I may.

Mairtin *takes his shovel and idles past* **Mick** *to Oona's grave.* **Mick** *stops work and looks at him threateningly.* **Mairtin** *taps the soil with his foot, then raises his shovel as if about to start digging.*

Mick One grain of that soil you touch, Mairtin Hanlon, it is *in* that grave you will be, not on it.

Mairtin *smiles, lays his shovel aside, and leans against the gravestone behind him.*

Mairtin Is it murder you're threatening now, Mick, and in earshot of your missus too?

Mick It isn't murder, because self-defence it would be, as protection from your wittering on like a fecking oul hen. I would be doing the community a service.

Mairtin The community a service? I heard you already did the community a service.

Mick What service?

Mairtin The community service you did, when they let you out of jail early.

Mick Now you're starting again.

Mick *returns to his digging.*

Mairtin I'm just saying, like.

Mick Now you're trying to come the clever.

Mairtin Well, as I say to Sheila Fahey, it isn't too hard I have to try to come the clever, because I *am* clever.

Mick Clever, is it? And is it ten times you've failed the Leaving Certificate now, or is it eleven times?

Mairtin It's one time.

Mick Oh, is it one time, now?

Mairtin The other time it coincided with me wrongful expulsion.

Mick Your wrongful expulsion? Uh-huh. The cat you cooked alive in biology?

Mairtin It wasn't me at all, now, Mick, and they knew full well it wasn't me, and didn't they have to reinstate me on the spot when Blind Billy Pender came out and confessed, with not a word of apology from them.

Mick Poor backward Blind Billy Pender, aye, whom you didn't influence in his confession at all.

Mairtin And it was a hamster anyways, if you would like to get your facts right.

Mick I don't need help from the likes of you to get me facts right.

Mairtin Oh aye.

Mick I'll tell you that anyways.

Mairtin (*pause*) Let's get a start on your missus's grave, Mick.

Mick (*pause*) We'll get a start when we've finished this one. And when the guard arrives.

Mairtin When the guard arrives? Oh. Is there a law, so, you can't dig up your wife unless you have the polis there?

Mick   Something of the like. Or, anyways, the guard had a word, said I'd best make sure he was there before we made a start. To save tongues wagging anyways.

Mairtin   What would tongues be wagging for?

Mick   I don't know. Just for the sake of it.

Sound of **Mick***'s shovel hitting the rotten wood at the bottom of the grave.*

Mairtin   Are you through to him?

Mick   Pass me the sack down.

Mairtin *jumps up from where he is and looks down into the grave. Sound of* **Mick** *jimmying rotten wood apart with his shovel. He picks the bits of wood up and throws them out of the grave.*
Mairtin *moves around a little to get a better view of the corpse.*

Mairtin   Ay yi yi, look at that one. Who is he? (*Glances behind.*) Daniel Faragher. Never heard of him.

Mick   I knew him to say hello to.

Mairtin   Would you recognise him?

Mick *looks at* **Mairtin** *as if he's stupid.*

Mairtin   Not from his bare skull, no, of course. Although he still has a lock of hair there, now. He looks like a big dolly.

Mick   A what?

Mairtin   A big dolly. Like girls do play with.

Mick   The girls won't be playing with this dolly.

Mairtin   I know that, sure. I'm only saying. How old would he be, then?

Mick   He would be . . .

Mairtin   No, let me guess, now.

Mick   Guess ahead.

Mairtin   A pound if I guess right.

Mick And a pound to me if you guess wrong.

Mairtin Okay. (*Glances at headstone and calculates.*) He was, I'd say . . . about sixty-seven now.

Mick Wrong. *Seventy*-seven he was. You owe me a pound.

Mairtin *looks back at the headstone again, recalculates on his fingers, and realises his mistake.*

Mairtin Ah feck.

Mick And pass me the sack, for the fiftieth time.

Mairtin *goes off mumbling behind the headstones.*

Mairtin I'll pass you the fecking sack . . .

. . . and returns with a large, dirty black cloth sack half-full of the bones and skulls of two corpses. **Mairtin** *passes it to* **Mick**.

Pass your skull to me, Mick. Just to compare, now.

Mick *hands* **Mairtin** *the skull with the lock of hair on it, then starts placing the bones from the grave into the sack, keeping a quiet eye on* **Mairtin** *all the while as he idles around with the skulls, placing them against his chest as if they're breasts at one point, kissing them together at another.*

Mairtin Sure skulls are great oul things. It's hard to believe you have one of these on the inside of your head.

Mick It's hard to believe *you* have one of them anyways, and the brain to go with it.

Mairtin I have no brain, is it? I have a brain too, and a big brain.

Mick Kissing skulls together. Like an oul schoolgirl.

Mairtin (*pause*) When do oul schoolgirls kiss skulls together, sure?

Mick (*pause*) I'm just saying, like.

Mairtin Oul schoolgirls can't get ahold of skulls at all.

He pokes a finger in the skulls' eye sockets.

You can stick your fingers right in their eyes.

Mick (*pause. Confused*) Oul schoolgirls' eyes, now?

Mairtin Skulls' eyes, now! Why would you be sticking your fingers in schoolgirls' eyes?

Mick I don't know, now.

Mairtin *hands the skulls back to* **Mick** *who places them in the sack, then quietly crouches down and looks into the grave.*

Mairtin Hey, Mick!

Mick What?

Mairtin Where does your thing go?

Mick Eh?

Mairtin Where does your thing go? When you die, I mean. None of them have had their things at all. And I've looked.

Mick I know well you've looked. And the women's too! I think that's why you came on this job, to have a good look. You don't see many living ones.

Mairtin I see my share.

Mick Of willies, now, Mairtin?

Mairtin Of the other, and you know well!

Mick Do you really not know where they go? Have you never been told?

Mairtin No.

Mick They don't tell you in religious studies?

Mairtin No. I do skip a lot of religious studies. It's just a lot of stuff about Jesus.

Mick That's the reason you don't know, so. Isn't it illegal in the Catholic faith to bury a body the willy still attached? Isn't it a sin in the eyes of the Lord?

Mairtin (*incredulous*) No . . .

Mick   Don't they snip them off in the coffin and sell them to tinkers as dog food.

Mairtin (*horrified*)   They do not!

Mick   And during the famine, didn't the tinkers stop feeding them to their dogs at all and start sampling the merchandise themselves?

Mairtin   They did not, now, Mick . . .

Mick   You would see them riding along with them, munching ahead.

Mairtin   No . . .

Mick   That's the trouble with young people today, is they don't know the first thing about Irish history.

Mick *smiles to himself.* **Mairtin**, *sickened, sees this and begins to doubt.*

Mairtin   That isn't true.

Mick   As true as I'm standing here.

Mairtin   I'll go up and ask oul Walsh, Welsh, at the church so. He'd be the man to know.

Mick   Go ahead, so.

Mairtin   Eh?

Mick   Go on ahead and ask for yourself.

Mairtin   I *will* go on ahead and ask.

Mick   Go so.

Mairtin (*pause*)   And ask do they cut the willies off and give them to tinkers?

Mick   Aye.

Mairtin (*pause*)   I'll go so.

Mick   So go.

Mairtin   I'm going. I don't need you to tell me to be going.

Mairtin *slowly idles off stage left.* **Mick** *smiles to himself when he's gone, then gets out of the grave he's in, having finished collecting its bones, lifts the sack out with him and puts it to one side. He idles over stage left to his wife's grave and looks down at it a while, hands in pockets. Enter the guard,* **Thomas Hanlon***, stage right, in full uniform, sucking on, at intervals throughout, a cigarette and an asthma inhaler.*

Thomas   You haven't started?

Mick   I haven't started.

Thomas   What are you doing so?

Mick   I'm just looking at it.

Thomas   Oh aye. No harm. I had some trouble out at the Riordan's Hall is why I'm late. Two women fighting and one man.

Mick   Was the two women fighting the man or who was fighting who?

Thomas   The two women was fighting among themselves and getting on fine when this oul fella butted in saying 'It's not right women fighting, break it up', and didn't the two of them deck him and take it in turns treading on him?

Mick   Good enough for him. What business was it of his them fighting. I like a good fight between women.

Thomas   The same as that, I like a good fight between women, although I couldn't say that while on duty, like. We arrested the lot of them anyways. The oul fella couldn't believe it. Went crying he did. Crying and wouldn't stop crying. And Johnny Doyle said 'I'll give you a batter too if you don't stop', but even then he wouldn't stop.

Mick   Did he give him a batter so?

Thomas   Ah no, now. There's no call to batter oul fellas, even if they're crying.

Mick   There's not I suppose.

Thomas   Ah no. Sure we'll be oul fellas too someday.

Mick (*pause*)   I'll get a start on this, so.

Thomas   Go ahead for yourself, aye.

Mick *starts digging up his wife's grave.* **Thomas** *sits against the right-hand headstone and looks inside the black sack, grimacing a little.*

Thomas   Awful morbid work this is, Mick.

Mick   It's work to be done.

Thomas   Awful ghoulish though.

Mick   Work to be done it is. Isn't the space needed?

Thomas   I'm certain there are other ways. Encouraging cremation is what the church should be. Not all this.

Mick   Who around here would go for cremation? No one.

Thomas   It's got to be better than this every year.

Mick   Get onto them so. (*Pause.*) Don't you come across more morbid things than this in your work every day? People only minutes dead you come across, neverminding seven years.

Thomas   When do I come across people only minutes dead?

Mick   Do you not? Oh. I thought the way you do talk about it, just like *Hill Street Blues* your job is. Bodies flying about everywhere.

Thomas   I would *like* there to be bodies flying about everywhere, but there never is.

Mick   Go ahead up north so. You'll be well away. Hang about a bookies or somewhere.

Thomas   Ah there's no detective work in that oul bullshit. Detective work I'm talking about. You know, like *Quincy*.

Mick   Oh, like *Quincy*. (*Pause.*) Have you never seen a dead body, so? A just dead body?

Thomas   The only body I've ever seen was a fella in a block of flats the road to Shannon. The fattest bastard you've ever seen in your life. Tits like this. Sitting, no clothes, in his armchair. No clothes, now. Television still on. A heart attack, the doctor said. All well and good. He knows more than me. But I had meself a look in that fat man's fridge, now. A mighty fridge it was, six feet high. What was in there? A pot of jam and a lettuce. Eh? And nothing else. A pot of jam and a lettuce in the fridge of the fattest man you've ever seen in your life. Nothing suspicious in that? I pointed it out in my report to them, and they just laughed at me. And watching television stark naked too? Nothing suspicious in that?

Mick (*pause*)   What time of year was it?

Thomas   What time of year? I don't know . . .

Mick   If it was the height of summer, and he wasn't expecting any visitors, it might very well explain the stark naked.

Thomas (*pause*)   It might explain the stark naked, aye. It might not explain the complete absence of food in his six-foot fridge! Eh?

Mick   You have a point.

Thomas   I have a point, aye. I know I have a point. The amount of food a fat fella eats? He won't get far on a lettuce and a pot of jam! Just laughed at me they did. (*Pause.*) Where's the young shite anyways?

Mick   Gone up to the church. I told him to ask the priest is it right the Church hands out the willies of the dead to passing tinker children to play with.

Thomas   And he hasn't gone?

Mick   He has gone.

Thomas   Oh he's as thick as five thick fellas, that fecker. What do they teach them in school now anyways?

Mick   I don't know what they teach them. Cooking cats they teach them.

Thomas Cooking cats, aye. No. A hamster it was.

Mick It's the same difference, sure.

Thomas Pardon me?

Mick It's the same difference, I said.

Thomas It's not the same difference at all, sure. A cat is one thing. A hamster is another.

Mick Is it worth the argue, now?

Thomas I'm just saying, like. (*Pause.*) A fact is a fact, like. It's the same in detective work. No matter how small a detail may appear to be, you can't go lumping it with a bunch of other details like it's all the same thing. So you can't go lumping cats and hamsters together either. Things like that are the difference between solving and not solving an entire case, sure.

Mick Oh aye, aye, they are, I suppose.

Mick *returns to his digging.*

Thomas They are. They certainly are. Oh aye. (*Pause.*) How far are you down?

Mick I'm down a good way. Funny, this soil's easy digging . . .

Mairtin *returns, angry, rubbing his cheek.*

Mairtin A back-fecking-hander the fecker gave me, you fecking bastard ya!

Mick *and* **Thomas** *laugh.*

Mairtin What the feck are yous laughing for, you feckers you?

Thomas Stop your cursing now, Mairtin. Not in the graveyard. Against God so it is.

Mairtin Against God, is it?

Thomas It is.

Mairtin Feck God so! And his mother too!

Both **Mick** *and* **Thomas** *stop to chastise* **Mairtin**, **Thomas** *standing.*

Mick Hey . . . ! !

Thomas Now, Mairtin, I'm liable to give you a batter meself if you go on like that, and a better batter it will be than the one you got from that biteen of a priest.

Mairtin Ah, go to blazes with you.

Thomas A bloody better batter it will be.

Mairtin Of course. Aren't the polis the experts at battering gasurs anyway? Don't you get a bonus for it?

Mick *continues digging.*

Thomas What gasurs do I ever batter?

Mairtin Ray Dooley for a start-off, or if not you then your bastarding cohorts.

Thomas What about Ray Dooley?

Mairtin Didn't he end up the County Hospital ten minutes after you arrested him?

Thomas He did, the pisshead, a broken toe. Kicking the cell door in and forgetting he had no shoes on him.

Mairtin Aye, that's what *you* say. That's what *you* say.

Thomas (*pause*) Don't be cursing God in a graveyard, anyway, is what the crux of the matter is.

Mairtin Aye, and don't be invading people's human rights is what the other crux of the matter is. The guards are there to serve the people, not the other way round, if you'd like to know.

Thomas You've been paying attention in Sociology class anyways, Mairtin.

Mairtin I have.

Thomas That's a good thing. Is it still Miss Byrne with the mini-skirts teaches that?

Mairtin I'm not bandying around pleasantries with the likes of you!

Mick Get back to fecking work, so, and start filling that one in.

Mairtin *tuts and goes to the right-hand grave with his shovel. He starts tipping the dirt back into it.*

Mairtin (*to* **Thomas**) I see you say nothing to him when he says 'feck' in the graveyard. Is it only kids, so you go shouting the odds with?

Thomas It is, aye. Only kids.

Mairtin I know well it is.

Thomas I do like to specialise.

Mairtin I know you do. (*Pause. Mumbling.*) Specialise me black arsehole.

As **Mairtin** *continues shovelling dirt at the grave's edge,* **Thomas** *quietly walks up behind him and shoves him down into it.* **Mairtin** *yelps.* **Mick** *and* **Thomas** *laugh, kicking dirt down onto him.* **Mairtin** *quickly clambers up from the rotten coffin underfoot.*

Mairtin You're a fecking fecker, Thomas. And you're nothing else.

Thomas (*laughing*) Haven't I told you, now, about your language?

Mairtin I'm going the feck home.

Thomas You're not going the feck home either. I've told dad to give you a batter himself if you're home before daybreak. So there you are.

Mairtin You're always ganging up on me, the fecking two of ye.

Thomas Ah, the babby's going crying now. Go on and help Mick, whiny, or I'll tell oul Welsh to be docking your wages on you.

Mairtin (*pause*) Do you need help with the digging there, Mick?

Mick No. Go on ahead with your filling in that one.

Mairtin *does so.* **Thomas** *lights a cigarette.*

Thomas (*pause*) Aren't you getting nervous there now, Mick? I'd be nervous, seeing me wife again after such a time.

Mick What's to be nervous for?

Mairtin Aye, what's to be nervous for?

Thomas Nothing at all, now.

Mick Nothing at all is right.

Thomas Aye, now. Only I thought you might have some things on your mind might be making you nervous seeing your missus again.

Mick What kind of things on me mind?

Mairtin Aye, what kind of things on his mind?

Thomas I don't know, now. I have no idea at all. Just things on your mind, like.

Mick I have no things on me mind.

Thomas Good-oh. I was just saying, like.

Mick What things are you saying I have on me mind?

Thomas No things at all, sure. None at all. Just conversing we are.

Mick Conversing me arse. Do you have something to say to me?

Thomas No, no, now . . .

Mick Because if you do, go ahead and spit it out. Is it me drink-driving you're saying?

Thomas   I was saying nothing, now, Mick.

Mick   Casting aspersions on me . . . ?

Thomas   I was casting no aspersions at all . . .

Mick   The family of eejits and blackguards you come from?

Mairtin (*pause*)   Who's an eejit and a blackguard? Is it me he's talking about, Thomas?

Thomas   It is, aye.

Mairtin (*pause*)   How do you know it's me he's talking about? It could've been you or dad or anybody he was talking about.

Thomas   Who were you talking about, Mick?

Mick   Him.

Thomas (*to* **Mairtin**)   See?

Mairtin   Ya feck!

Thomas   Now, Mick, you've insulted poor wee Mairtin there, you've insulted family, such as it is, so now I have to go and say something insulting back to you. That is the way that these things operate.

Mick   You're the one who started with the insults.

Thomas   No, Mick, no. I have to take you up on that. You're the one who started with the insults. I was the one who started with the vague insinuations.

Mick   It's the self-same thing.

Thomas   Pardon me?

Mick   It's the self-same thing, I said.

Thomas   It's not the self-same thing at all, and if you knew anything about the law then you'd know it's not the self-same thing. So now I have to turn me vague insinuations into something more of an insult, so then we'll all be quits . . .

Mairtin (*to* **Mick**)   Your ma was a queer and your da was a queer and how they came up with you is a mystery of the Universe!

Both **Mick** *and* **Thomas** *stare blankly at* **Mairtin** *for a few moments, who looks away, embarrassed. Pause.*

Thomas   No, what I was going to say was . . . some insinuation along the lines of . . . not that I'm making any accusations, mind . . . but maybe your wife's head injuries all those years ago weren't especially conducive to only having been in a car crash at all, and maybe . . .

Mick (*angrily*)   All that came out at the time, Thomas Hanlon, and didn't the inquest shoot every word of it down!

Thomas   Y'know, maybe she was already dead *before* you drove her into the wall, that kind of insinuation, like. But nothing harsher than that am I saying,

Mick   Take all of that back, Thomas Hanlon!

Thomas   I'm only suggesting, now, like.

Mick   Take every word of it back, because if you make me get up out of this grave, now, polis or not . . .

Thomas   You take eejit and blackguard back, so, and I'll be pleased to take it back.

Mick   You take your things back first.

Thomas   No, now. You said your things first, so it's only fair you take them back first too.

Mick   There was no call for any of this.

Thomas   I agree with you, like.

Mick   For any of these insults. (*Pause.*) I take eejit and blackguard back.

Thomas   I take wife-butcherer back, so.

Mairtin *laughs loudly, half in surprise, half in pride, as* **Mick** *and* **Thomas** *stare at each other.*

Mairtin Is that all true?

Mick A pure drink-driving it was, Thomas, and you know full well it was.

Thomas I *do* know full well it was, and I've taken me accusations back without reservation.

Mairtin Is it true, Thomas?

Thomas Of course it's not true, Mairtin. Haven't I just said? I made up every word of it.

Mairtin (*confused*) I thought you were saying it was true.

Thomas Not at all. A pure drink-driving is all it was, just like Mick says.

Mick *and* **Thomas** *stare at each other a few seconds more, then* **Mick** *returns to his digging.*

Mairtin Oh-h. I'm disappointed so.

Thomas Why are you disappointed, babby?

Mairtin There you got me hoping I was working with a fella up and slaughtered his wife with an axe or something, when all it was was an oul cheap-ass drink-driving. Aren't they ten-a-penny? Wouldn't it be hard to find somebody round here who *hasn't* killed somebody drink-driving? Or if not a somebody then a heifer, or at least a dog. Didn't oul Marcus Rigby kill twins with his tractor, and him over seventy?

Thomas No, he did not.

Mairtin Did he not? Who was it killed twins with his tractor so? It was someone.

Thomas No. That was just something I told you when you was twelve to mind you kept out of the road with your bicycle when you saw a tractor coming.

Mairtin (*pause*) There was no twins at all?

Thomas If you had any sense you'd have known when did ever twins live around here?

Mairtin Twins come over from America I was thinking, to see where *The Quiet Man* was filmed and got lost.

Thomas You was thinking wrong, so. I only said twins to get you thinking if a tractor killed two gasurs it'd be twice as likely a tractor'd kill you, there only being one of you.

Mairtin (*angrily*) So all those years I drove me bicycle through hedgerows and banks of skitter and all on account of them poor mangled twins I had on me mind, and it was all for nothing?!

Thomas (*laughing*) It was, indeed.

Mairtin You're a bastard of a bastard of a bastard of a feck, Thomas Hanlon!

Thomas You're still alive anyways, is the main thing. Do you know how many boys the age of eight died falling into slurry tanks the last year in Ireland alone?

Mairtin I don't! And I don't fecking care!

Thomas Fourteen. Fourteen of the poor gasurs.

Mairtin Good! And let them die!

Thomas And drowning in slurry, Mairtin beag, isn't the nicest way to go out of this world. I'll tell you that for yourself.

Mairtin Feck drowning in slurry, and feck their mothers too . . . !

Mick (*interrupting*) That's not true, now, is it, Thomas? The fourteen gasurs drowning in the slurry?

Thomas It *is* true, aye. (*Pause.*) Not altogether, mind . . .

Mick No.

Thomas Not all in the one tank, now. Separately.

Mick Separately. In different parts of the country, like, and at different times.

Thomas   Aye. From the Central Office of Statistics this is. They have good statistics they do. More kids die in slurry tanks than die in combine harvesters. Only seven died in combine harvesters.

Mick   Of course. Because more people have slurry tanks than have combine harvesters.

Thomas   That's true enough.

Mick   It's only rich people have combine harvesters. And their kids are less thick anyways.

Thomas   Is right.

Mick   To go climbing in slurry you have to be thick.

Thomas   You do.

Mairtin (*angrily*)   It wasn't climbing in slurry this conversation was at all! This conversation was the lie about the dead twins!

As he speaks, **Thomas** *pushes* **Mairtin** *over into the grave again and kicks dirt at him.*

Thomas   Ah, shut your creeping bollocks about the dead twins, ya fecking oul shite-arse ya, and you're nothing else.

Mairtin   Kick dirt at me, is it?! And . . . and call me an oul shite-arse, is it?!

Thomas   It is. You observed well.

Mairtin   We'll see about that so, you fecker . . .

Thomas   Oh aye, now. The babby's angry . . .

Mairtin *starts clambering up out of the side of the grave to get at* **Thomas,** *who takes his truncheon out in readiness. Just as* **Mairtin** *gets to his feet, the sound of* **Mick***'s shovel splintering the rotten coffin lid under his feet is heard.*

Mick   I'm through to it.

Mairtin *and* **Thomas** *stare at each other a moment, then forget their fight and go and stand over* **Mick** *at the grave.* **Mick** *crouches* *down, so he's almost out of sight, to pull up the rotten boards.*

Thomas Prepare yourself so, Mick, now. She'll be a shock to you.

Mick The boards are ... funny. The boards are already broke open, or is that just the rot, now?

Mick *throws a couple of bits of rotten board away.*

Thomas Dig some more of that dirt off there, Mick.

Mick *takes his shovel and scrapes some more of the dirt from the coffin. After a few seconds, his scraping starts becoming more frantic.*

Mick What's the ... ? What's the ... ?

Thomas Is she ... ?

Mairtin This is a peculiar business.

Mick *throws the shovel away and ducks down into the grave again, this time desperately scraping the dirt away with his bare hands.*

Mick (*frantic*) Where is she ... ?! Where is she ... ?!

Thomas (*quietly*) Is she not ... ?

Mick (*shouting, voice almost breaking*) She's not there!

His scraping ceases. Pause. He stands back up, dirty and bedraggled, looking down into the grave numbly.

(*Quietly.*) She's not there.

Pause. Blackout.

Scene Three

Night, a day or two later. Set the same as in Scene One. Three skulls and their sets of bones lie on the table in front of **Mairtin** *who stares dumbly down at them, swaying, drunk, blowing bubbles. He has a mallet in one hand and a quarter-empty bottle of poteen in the other, from which he takes disgusted sips every now and then.* **Mick** *can be heard rummaging through a toolbox offstage. He is also drunk.*

Mick (*off*) There's another one here somewhere I know.

Mairtin What do you be wanting an oul woody hammer for, Mick, now?

Mick They do call them mallets.

Mairtin Ohh. (*Pause.*) Skulls do be more scary on your table than they do be in their coffin. Why? I don't know why. Some reason now.

Mick Are you getting scared, you wee pup?

Mairtin I'm not getting scared at all. All right I'm getting a bit scared. You won't be leaving me on me own more long?

Mick The minute I find this feck I'll be with you. No chance of you helping me look.

Mairtin (*absently*) No. (*Pause.*) Weren't they terrible heathens whoever pinched your missus on you?

Mick They were. And if I ever got me hands on the fecks, then we'd see.

Mairtin What would you do to them, Mick? Would you give them a kick?

Mick It would be worse than a kick.

Mairtin Would you peg stones at them?

Mick Worse than stones it'd be.

Mairtin Peg ... biteens'a ... rocks ...

Mick You wouldn't have heard tell of who took her, Mairtin? Not one of your oul mates, I'm thinking?

Mairtin None of my mates. What would one of my mates be wanting with your oul missus? My mates don't be fooling with dead missuses.

Mick And can we rule you off the list of suspects too?

Mairtin I'm on no list of suspects. If I was to be digging up your missus it's good money I'd be wanting for the job, the same as you, cash in hand. Maybe it was a set of tinkers dug her up on you.

Mick   What would tinkers be wanting with her?

Mairtin   I don't know. Maybe they were expecting another praitie blight and felt like something to be munching on ahead of time. Not that there'd be much to munch on with your missus. No willy anyways. As far as I know anyways, I didn't know the woman. I still can't believe that about them willies. That's an awful thing.

Mick   Found the feck!

Mick *enters, a half-empty bottle of poteen in one hand, a mallet in the other, which he shows to* **Mairtin**.

Mairtin   What will be playing so, Mick? That oul game with the hoops and the sticks they do play in England with the hoops and the sticks and the balls they do play in England, what's it called, with the hoops and the sticks? They do play it in England. It has a 'c'.

Mick   Are you looking in me eyes now, Mairtin?

Mairtin   What eyes?

Mick   *My* eyes.

Mairtin   Aye, your eyes. *Croquet!*

Mick   Did you have anything to do with my wife going missing?

Mairtin   Eh?

Mick   Did you have anything to do with my wife going missing?

Mairtin   No.

Mick *keeps staring at* **Mairtin** *for a long time, as* **Mairtin** *sways slightly but returns the stare.*

Mick   You have looked me in the eyes and I believe you now, Mairtin. I do apologise for even asking you.

Mairtin   Good-oh.

Mick *shakes* **Mairtin** *by the hand and walks over to the table.*

Mick   Are these skulls still scaring you?

Mairtin   I'm less scared now but don't be leaving me on me own again with them. When they get me on me own they do go smiling at me. Especially that one.

Mick   Shall we be teaching them a lesson then so?

Mairtin   Sure you can't teach skulls lessons. They have no brain to be sticking the . . . lesson . . .

Mick   Knowledge?

Mairtin   Knowledge. They have no brain to be sticking the lesson through the holes knowledge into.

Mick   This is the only lesson skulls be understanding.

He brings the mallet crashing down on the skull nearest to him, shattering it, spraying pieces of it all over the room.

He won't be smiling no more.

Mairtin   You've buggered him to skitter!

Mick   I have. Not skitter enough.

Mick *starts smashing the skull into even smaller pieces and stamping on the bits that have fallen on the floor.* **Mairtin** *stares at him dumbfounded.*

Mairtin   Ease them in the lake you said.

Mick   In front of the fat one I said, aye. Batter the shite out of them is nearer the mark. And why not? If it's whispering about me they're going to be through the years, what more should they expect when they wind up in my hands than batter?

Mairtin   Nothing more.

Mick   Nothing more is right.

Mairtin   May I be having a batter, Mick? Ah let me now.

Mick   Why else have I invited you here with a hammer in your hand?

Mairtin   I can? Ohh Jeebies ... Goodbye Daniel Faragher. You've been smiling at me long enough, boy.

Mairtin *takes a little run-up and starts smashing another of the skulls and its bones to pieces. The smashing continues more or less unabated by at least one of the men throughout most of the rest of the scene.*

Mick   That one's Biddy Curran, not Dan Faragher at all.

Mairtin   Biddy Curran, ya currant bun, ya ...

Mick   She was a fat oul bitch.

Mairtin   She's thin enough now, God bless her. And getting more thin.

Mick   The middle one's Dan, and Dan's mine.

Mick *starts smashing the middle skull.*

Mairtin   Ar, you've done two and I've only done one, Mick, ya snatching feck.

Mick   Don't be going crying, Mairtin. And haven't you had half a bottle of poteen off me today if I'm such a snatching feck?

Mairtin   I have. (*Drinks.*) You're not a snatching feck at all. You're a generous man.

Mick   You can join in with Dan's bones if you like.

Mairtin   I'll be taking a pop at Biddy Curran's pelvis and then I'll see how I'm feeling.

Mick   Good-oh.

Mairtin   Should you not be putting a whatyoucall down to be catching them?

Mick   What matter?

Mairtin   Or a thing?

Mick   If you'll not be liking my skull-battering ways you can be off with you.

Mairtin   Your ways is fine indeed.

Mick   I do have a dustpan and brush.

Mairtin   I was thinking. Goodbye Biddy Curran or whatever it is your name is. You're all mixed up now anyways, you poor feck you.

Mick   Don't be cursing now, Mairtin.

Mairtin   I won't be.

Mick   Not when you're handling the departed, now.

Mairtin   This is more fun than hamster-cooking!

Mick   It is. Or if it is I don't know. I've never cooked hamsters.

Mairtin   I've only cooked one hamster. It's not all it's cracked up to be. You stick him in alive and he comes out dead. The feck hardly squeals . . . I mean, the fella hardly squeals. If the oven had had a see-through door it would've been more fun, but it didn't, it had an ordinary door. My mistake was not planning ahead. I was egged on. But this is more fun. Is skull-hammering more fun than wife-into-wall-driving, Mick?

Mick   Oh Mairtin, you're getting a bit near to the mark there, boy.

Mairtin   Oh I am. When I drink I do get awful stupid. I apologise, Mick.

Mick   I accept your apology, Mairtin. Seeing as you're drunk as Jaysus.

Mairtin   I *am* drunk as Jaysus. But I'll be putting me head in a bucket of water when I get home and I'll be fine then. I do do that of a Saturday night I do, and me dad does never twig I've been drinking.

Mick   Be remembering to take your head out of the bucket afterwards is the main thing.

Mairtin   I know. Else you'd go drowning.

Mick   Is right.

Mairtin *stops hammering abruptly, to launch into his story, and* **Mick** *stops quickly also, to listen.*

Mairtin   Did my brother ever tell you the drunk out in Salthill, lay down on the floor to sleep, and where was his head resting? His head was resting in a potty of wee. Drowned he did! On wee! Eh?

Mick   On wee, was it?

Mairtin   Drowned on wee. What a way to go, eh?

Mick   Was it his own wee?

Slight pause.

Mairtin   I don't know if it was his own wee or not. And I don't care. He drowned on wee is all I'm saying.

Mick   No, now. A fact like that is very important, now. Your brother would be the first to agree.

Mairtin (*pause*)   Now that I think of it, I think my brother *did* want to launch an investigation into the matter, but they wouldn't let him. But I don't know if it was whose wee it was was what aroused his suspicions or not. Sure, a pig that smelt would arouse that bastard's suspicions. Thinks he's Starsky and Hutch. (*Pause.*) I, for one, would rather drown on me own wee than on anybody else's. Though I'd rather not drown on wee at all!

Mick   I had three uncles drowned on sick.

Mairtin (*pause*)   But, sure, drowned on sick is nothing to go shouting about. Doesn't everybody drown on sick?

Mick   Three uncles now, I'm saying.

Mairtin   Three uncles or no. Drowned on sick is ten-a-penny now, Mick. A million have drowned on sick. Oul black fella. Jimi Hendrix. Drowned on sick. Drowned on wee I'm talking about. Drowned on wee you have to go out of your way. Drowned on sick you don't. And of course. Sick is there in your gob already. Wee is nowhere near.

Mick If it's drunk you are and you go to bed and you fear you may be sick, this is what you should do . . .

He lays down flat on his belly on the floor, his face to one side.

Lay down flat on your belly or on your side, your face turned to the side of the pillow. Or throw the pillow away completely would be the best thing.

Mairtin I don't need advice from you, Mick Dowd, on not drowning on sick. I know well.

Mick Like this, now.

Mairtin I know like that, and your floor is filthy.

Mick This is what I always remember on going to bed, no matter how much of a sup I've had, this is what I always remember (*Almost tearfully.*) in mind of me three poor uncles, were young men.

Mairtin Get up anyways, now, because it wasn't sick was the subject at all. You do always be changing the subject on me. Wee was the subject.

Mick (*getting up*) Three uncles, I'm saying.

Mairtin I know, three uncles.

Mick And one of them in America.

Mairtin In America? I suppose people do drown on their sick in America too. Oh of course.

Mick In Boston Massachusetts.

Mairtin In Boston Massachusetts?

Mick In Boston Massachusetts. He did drown on his sick.

Mairtin I suppose at least he'd travelled. (*Pause.*) Good-oh.

The two almost simultaneously begin smashing up the bones again.

Mick   We should have music as we're doing this.

Mairtin (*blankly*)   Music, music . . .

Mick   Music to hammer dead fellas to. I have a Dana record somewhere . . .

Mairtin   Put Dana on so.

Mick *puts on 'All Kinds of Everything' by Dana.*

Mick   I didn't think young people liked Dana nowadays.

Mairtin   They may not but I do. I've liked Dana since I was a child. If I met Dana I'd give her a kiss.

Mick   She wouldn't be kissing you, ya get.

Mairtin   For why?

Mairtin *stops hammering, looking sad and serious.* **Mick** *stops and looks at him.*

Mick   Why wouldn't Dana be kissing you?

Mairtin   Aye.

Mick (*pause*)   Well maybe she would, now.

Mairtin   On the lips.

Mick (*shrugging*)   Maybe she would.

Mairtin   Although she's a born-again Christian now.

Mick   Honestly, Mairtin, I'd avoid her.

Mick *starts hammering again, and after a few seconds* **Mairtin** *joins him.*

Mairtin (*pause*)   Would you be hammering your missus's bones with equal fervour were she here, Mick?

Mick   I wouldn't be. I'd have some respect.

Mairtin   Maybe a favour it was they did you so, the

fellas went and stole her on you?

Mick No favour was it to me, and if I had the feckers here, then you'd be seeing some fancy skull-battering. I'll tell you that. Battered to dust they would be!

Mairtin Good enough for them, the morbid oul fecks. And not only stealing your missus then, if that weren't enough, but to go pinching the locket that lay round her neck too, a locket that wouldn't fetch you a pound in the Galway pawn, I'd bet.

Mick *has stopped hammering on the locket's first mention and stepped back a pace, staring at* **Mairtin** *whose hammering continues unabated, entirely unaware of his faux-pas.*

Mick The rose locket, was it?

Mairtin The rose locket, aye, with the picture of you. What use would the fecks have in taking that, other than just to taunt you?

Mick *sits down in the armchair, the mallet in his lap, still staring at* **Mairtin**, *who continues ahead with the skulls.*

Mairtin The miserable heathen gets, and that's all they are. It was probably the same ones stole me *Star Wars* men on me when I was four, when I left them out in the rain. It was Han and Luke and ... was it Chewie? No, I didn't have Chewie. It was Han and Luke and some other one they had off me ... Princess Leia! Aye, and them are the three best ones in *Star Wars*. You can't play *Star Wars* without them. Look at you sitting there! Be getting back to work you, ya slack feck ya, or I'll have a word with oul Welsh Welsh to be docking your wages on you. Welsh.

Mick In a minute now, Mairtin. I've to sit down and be having a think a minute.

Mairtin (*stopping hammering*) That's what all the clever kids at school do do is sit down and be having a think, when it's out in the yard playing football they should be, and getting some sun on their arms. You can't budge the freckle-faced fecks, not even with a dig. (*Pause.*) Ah good luck to them, they're not harming anyone. Why should I be ordering them about and giving them digs? They've every right to be sitting. (*Pause.*) I do get in an awful happy mood when it's out of me brains I am, Mick.

Mick I can see.

Mairtin I could kiss fools and feck dogs. (*Pause.*) Have we done enough hammering for the meantime so?

Mick We have.

Mairtin What's next on the agenda?

Mick Be picking up a few of the big lumps, there, and be putting them in the sack.

Mairtin *does so, drunkenly.*

Mairtin Ah there's too many of the bastards to be picking up. You should get a hoover.

Mick Just a few more of the big ones will do us.

Mairtin I was promised a dustpan and brush a while back. I see that promise proved untrue. Now what?

Mick (*standing*) Now we'll be driving them out to the lake to be starting the disposing.

Mairtin With a string of prayers said over them, Mick?

Mick With a string of prayers said over them. I'll be getting me car out now, unless I don't suppose you'd want to be driving, Mairtin?

Mairtin Ah you wouldn't let me be driving, would ya?

Mick If you're not up to the job, no I wouldn't be.

Mairtin I'd be up to the job, Mick! I'd be up to the job!

Mick You're not a tadeen over the limit, now?

Mairtin I'm not near the limit, sure. I've had a bare sip. Oh let me be driving, Mick. Please now.

Pause. **Mick** *takes his car keys out of his pocket and tosses them to*

Mairtin, *who fumbles them at length and drops them, then drunkenly picks them back up off the floor.*

Mairtin Oh jeebies, this has turned into a great oul night. Driving and drinking and skull-battering . . .

Mairtin *dashes out through the front door, leaving his sack behind him.*

Mick Be bringing your bag of skulleens now, Mairtin!

Pause. **Mairtin** *returns slowly, smiling, and picks up the sack.*

Mairtin I'd forget me head if it wasn't screwed up. *On.* Me mam does say 'You'd forget your head you would, Mairtin.' I say oh aye.

He exits with sack.

(*Off.*) I'll be sure and remember to be putting me seat-belt on too, Mick, knowing your track record.

Sound of **Mairtin** *laughing, off.*

Mick (*quietly*) Be doing what you like, ya feck . . .

He picks up his mallet and rolls it around in his hand a little.

It'll make no difference in the end.

He exits briskly, bringing the mallet with him and turning the lights off behind him, as the sound of a car starting up is heard.

Scene Four

Mick *enters, turns lights on. His shirt is covered in blood. He wipes some blood off his mallet and lays it on the table, then brushes the bone fragments littering the floor into the next room. He sits in his armchair when finished. There is a knock at the door.* **Mick** *lets* **Maryjohnny** *in.*

Mary Mick.

Mick Maryjohnny.

Mary Cold.

Mick I suppose it's cold.

Mary Oh, now, it's cold, Mick.

Mick Well, it's *night* I suppose.

Mary Oh it's night, aye.

Mick I suppose a sup would you be after?

Mary Ah only if you're having one, Mick, now.

Mick *pours them two glasses.*

Mary I've just come from the bingo.

Mick Oh aye, and how many times tonight did you win?

Mary Only three times tonight, Mick. One of me flourescent pens ran out on me.

Mick Uh-huh, that's always the worry with flourescent pens. You had a bad night of it so.

Mary Two free goes on the bumpy slides at the Leisureland swimming is all they gave me. I won't get much use out of them. (*Pause.*) You wouldn't want them, Mick?

Mick I wouldn't, Mary. I was never a man for bumpy slides. Never saw the sense in them.

Mary I'll give them to Mairtin or someone so. Is Mairtin able to swim?

Mick *wipes some of the blood from himself.*

Mick I'd bet money against it.

Mary What's all that on you, Mick? Out painting have you been?

Mick I have, aye. I've been out painting red things.

Mary That'll stain.

Mick Ah it's just an oul work-shirt, Maryjohnny. What harm?

Mary   No harm. (*Pause.*) I heard tell of your Oona going missing on you, Mick. That was a terrible thing. If you can't be let rest when it's seven years dead you are, when can you be let rest.

Mick   You can never be let rest.

Mary   I couldn't bear to think of anyone running off with my bones when I'm dead.

Mick   No one'll run off with your bones, Maryjohnny. Sure, they'd need a small truck to begin with.

Mary   A small truck for why?

Mick   No why. Just a biteen big-boned sometimes you do seem.

Mary   I'm not big-boned. I'm just a bit fat is all.

Mick   A bit fat, oh aye, aye. A bit fat indeed.

Mary   It's a peculiar mood tonight you're in, Mick.

Mick   It is. It must be them paint fumes or something.

Mary (*pause*)   Did you hear Ray Dooley's lost his tour guide job?

Mick   I did. Sure, if you go pegging shite at Americans you're bound to lose your tour guide job.

Mary   You are.

Mick   And cracking Vietnam jokes then.

Mary   Off to Boston for his brother's wedding next month he is.

Mick   Next month, is it? That wasn't a very long engagement. Me and Oona five years we were engaged, and it was five years we well needed. To get to know each other's faults and the like, y'know, and to accept them then.

Mary   What was Oona's biggest fault, Mick?

Mick   Oona didn't have big faults really. She just had

little faults. Niggly things, y'know? She'd never wrap up
cheese properly. Y'know, when she was finished with it.
She'd just leave it lying about, letting the air get to it. The
same with bread. She'd never wrap up bread properly.
Y'know, like after she'd made a sandwich or the like. And
she was terrible at scrambled eggs, and I don't know why,
because scrambled eggs are easy to do. Oona's scrambled
eggs'd come out either grey or burned.

Mary   You don't miss her so.

Mick   I *do* miss her. I mean, that scrambled egg business
wasn't really a big thing. We'd just avoid having scrambled
eggs, y'know? (*Pause.*) I miss the talk of her. Oona could fill
the house with talk. And she'd always stand up for me
against people. Y'know, in a fight or something, or if
people were saying things agin me. She'd've been the first
to defend me if she heard the town was saying I murdered
her on purpose.

Mary   It's a shame she's dead so. (*Pause.*) I wonder who it
was took her?

Mick   Uh-huh?

Thomas *knocks and enters, carrying a small bag.*

Mary   Evening, Thomas. Cold.

Thomas   What are you doing up here?

Mary   I was passing on me way from the bingo.

Thomas   I thought I told Father Welsh to bar you from
the bingo.

Mary   You did but Father Welsh reinstated me to the
bingo.

Thomas   So he countermanded official police orders, did
he? I'll have to be looking into that one. You run along
home now, Gran. I want to speak to Mick alone.

Mary   I've only just got here, sure.

Thomas   I don't care if you've only just got here. That's an official police order, I'm saying.

Mary   Don't you go official police ordering me, Thomas Hanlon, the number of times I wiped the dribbling skitter off the bare babby's backside of ya.

Thomas   *Please*, Gran.

Mary   I'll go when I've finished me sup and not before.

Mick   What would you want to be speaking to me alone for anyways?

Thomas   Oh nothing terrible important really. Just I'd like you to write out and sign a little oul confession for me, that's all. Just a weeny little confession, like.

Mick   A confession to what?

Thomas *takes a skull with a large forehead-crack out of his bag.*

Thomas   A confession to the murdering be blunt instrument, or be some sort, of instrument, of your late wife, Mrs Oona Margaret Dowd.

Thomas *gestures to the skull crack.*

Mary   No ... !

Mick   Oh. Okay so.

Thomas   Hah?

Mick   Okay, I said. Do ya have a pen?

Thomas *(checks himself)*   I don't. Don't you have one?

Mick *looks for a pen.*

Mick   I have one somewhere, I know.

Mary *(takes out bingo pens)*   I have me bingo pens. They're flourescent but they don't all work.

Thomas   Sure flourescent pens are no good for filling out confessions, sure!

Mary   A yalla one?

Thomas No. 'A yalla one', Jesus.

Mick (*finding pen*) Here, me lucky lotto pen. Now, what exactly do you want me to be saying, Thomas?

Thomas Well, the *truth*, Mick.

Mick Oh, the truth, aye. Fair enough.

Mick *writes out his confession on two pieces of paper* **Thomas** *gives him, as* **Mary** *picks the skull up.*

Mary It's true? (*Pause.*) I had always prayed only fool gossiping is all it ever was. If I had known that . . .

Mick If you had known that you'd still've come up cadging booze off me all these years, ya cheapskate fecking lump.

Thomas Don't you go calling my granny a cheapskate fecking lump, ya murdering oul ghoul, ya.

Mick Murdering oul what ya?

Thomas Ghoul, ghoul.

Mick Oh, ghoul. I thought you said 'whore'.

Thomas And don't go criticising me pronunciation either!

Mick (*to* **Mary**) You just put my wife's skull down now you, you and your flourescent fecking pens. Look at as many flourescent pens she has, Thomas, when bingo's supposed to be a bit of fun and a bit of fun to raise a few bob for them poor oul fecks in Africa. Out the mouths of starving darkies Maryjohnny rips her bingo winnings, but I see you don't go getting her confessing.

Mary Isn't it better to starve darkies than to murder missuses?

Mick Not at all is it better, and put my Oona down now, you, I've told you once. I don't want the pooh-stench of your manky hands grubbing all over her.

Mary *puts skull down and continues drinking.* **Mick** *writes.*

Mick Where was it you found her, Thomas?

Thomas Down the bottom of our fields I found her.

Mick The bottom of ye're fields, oh aye. Down beside
the bones of that dead cow Mairtin was telling us about the
other day, I'll bet. The one he said wandered in and fell
down dead, when doesn't the world and his wife know he
dragged that cow screaming from Pato Dooley's place and
hit it with a brick, and it's only as easy-going as Pato is he
never pressed charges.

Thomas That's only circumstantial evidence.

Mick No, that's only *hearsay* evidence.

Thomas Feck I'm always getting them two beggars
mixed up. What harm? It isn't knowing the difference
between hearsay and circumstantial evidence that makes
you a great copper. No. Detective work it is, and going
hunting down clues, and never letting a case drop no
matter what the odds stacked against you, no matter how
many years old.

Mary Like *Petrocelli*.

Thomas Like *Petrocelli* is right, Gran, and the first thing I
do when they promote me is reopen the case of that lettuce
and jam man I was telling you about, 'cos I can't sleep
nights sometimes thinking of that poor fella's murder going
four years unsolved, as cold and alone in his big fat grave
he lies.

Mick And the fella who drowned on wee is another.

Thomas And the fella who drowned on wee is another. I
may bring a urine expert in on that one.

Mick What's another word for 'convulse'? I've used
'convulse' once and I don't want to be repeating meself.

Thomas (*thinking*) Convulse, convulse, convulse . . .
Spasm.

Mick Spasm, spasm, spasm . . . Good one. (*Writes.*)

Thomas   I have a great vocabulary me, I do, oh aye. (*Pause.*) Are you nearly done?

Mick   I'm nearly done, all right.

Mary   Poor Oona. Why did you kill her, Mick? Sure, bad scrambled eggs is no just cause to butcher your wife.

Mick   I know it's not, Mary, and do you want to hear something funny? I *didn't* butcher my wife. Just like for seven long years I've been saying I didn't butcher my wife. I never butchered anybody 'til tonight.

He gives his confession to **Thomas**, *who reads through it at speed.*

A pure, drink-driving was all my Oona was, as all along I've said, but if it's a murderer ye've always wanted living in yere midst, ye can fecking have one.

Thomas   D'you think I'm going to believe this pile of fecking bull?! Down the disco with Ray Dooley tonight Mairtin is, and nowhere but the disco.

Mick   But, sure, if down the disco Mairtin was, how would I have ended up with his bastard brains dripping down the bloody front of me?

Mary   No . . . !

Mick   D'you see how great a copper he is, Maryjohnny, with his skulls and his solving and his lettuces in empty fridges, yet doesn't bat an eye at a blood-soaked man standing whap-bang in front of the feck-brained fool . . .

Thomas *dives for* **Mick**, *knocking him off his chair and strangling him on the floor,* **Mick** *barely defending himself.*

Mary   Leave him, Thomas, leave him! Thomas!

Mairtin *enters behind her, somewhat concussed, a big bloody crack down the centre of his forehead, dripping onto his shirt. He watches the fight a while,* **Mary** *noticing him after a few seconds, confused.*

Mairtin   What are them two gobshites up to?

Thomas *stops strangling* **Mick**. *Both stand and stare at* **Mairtin**.

Mairtin What are ye's feckers looking at? Ye's *fellas* looking at, I mean?

Thomas *examines* **Mairtin***'s wound.* **Mary** *sits, refilling drink.*

Mary How are you, Mairtin?

Mairtin I'm fine, Gran, although a biteen of a headache I do have, aye. What are you doing pawing at me, you?

Thomas *rubs* **Mairtin***'s face gently.*

Thomas We have you now, Michael Dowd. We have you now.

Thomas *takes his handcuffs out and goes to* **Mick***.*

Mairtin Have him for what?

Thomas Have him for ramming a mallet through the poor brains of you.

Mairtin A mallet? What are you talking about, sure? A pure drink-driving is all this was.

Thomas Hah?

Mick Hah?

Mairtin A pure drink-driving is all this was. What would Mick want to go malleting my poor brains for? Mick likes me an awful lot, don't you, Mick?

Mick I do, Mairtin. Sure I think you're a great fella.

Mairtin See, Thomas? Mick thinks I'm a great fella.

Behind **Thomas***'s back,* **Mick** *picks up the confession and sets it alight. It slowly burns as* **Thomas** *questions* **Mairtin***.*

Thomas Listen, Mairtin, concussed is all you are now, and who wouldn't be . . .

Mairtin I'm not at all concussed. It'd take more than a major car-crash to concuss me, I'll tell ya.

Thomas But didn't he just sign a confession saying he

hacked through the drunken skull of ya?

Mairtin   Did ya, Mick?

Mick   No, no, I didn't, Mairtin.

Mairtin   There you go.

Thomas   What d'you mean you didn't? Don't I have the fecking thing right here . . . ?

Thomas *turns to see the last corner of the confession burning to ash.*

Mick   You've cocked it up again, haven't ya?

Thomas   Mairtin? Listen to me. You're going to come down to the station with me, now, and you're going to swear out how Mick it was tried to kill you tonight . . .

Mairtin   Oh Jesus, can't you just leave poor Mick alone and in peace, you, *McMillan and Wife*?

Thomas   Don't keep calling me *McMillan and Wife*, I've told you twenty fecking times!

Mairtin   If he said he didn't kill his missus that's good enough for me, and let it rest.

Thomas   What are you on his fecking side for?!

Mairtin   Well why wouldn't I be on his fecking side, when it's me own blackguard brother I catch carving a hole in Mick's missus's skull there, the day after you'd dug her up on him.

Thomas   Shut up about that digging . . . !

Mairtin   I won't shut up about that digging and I'll tell you why I won't shut up about that digging! Because not even a fecking pound would the Galway pawn give me for that rose locket, and you said it'd get me at least ten.

He gives **Mick** *the locket.*

Only gave me that to shut me up, he did, Mick, but I realise that'd be nothing more than stealing from ya, and

not only stealing from ya but stealing from the poor dead
wife of ya, and anyways the fella in the pawn said it was
just a piece of shite not worth pissing on, so it's no great
loss, ya know what I mean, like?

Thomas Are you finished, Mairtin?

Mairtin (*pause. Confused*) Am I Finnish?

Thomas Are you *finished*, I said.

Mairtin Oh, am I finished? (*Thinks awhile.*) No I'm not
finished, Mr high-and-mighty detective bollocks. Heh,
detective me arse, when the whole of Leenane knows you'd
have trouble arresting a shop-lifting child, if the child
confessed with the chocolate round his gob. Or if you did
arrest him you'd arrest him for killing the Kennedys.

Thomas Is that right?

Mairtin It is. Sure it's only 'cos you're so good at
helping kids across the road that you're even tolerated in
this job.

Thomas You're finished now, are ya?

Mairtin I'm finished for the minute, aye, but I may be
thinking up some more insults for ya in a whileen once I
get me breath back.

Thomas But for the time being you're finished?

Mairtin For the time being I'm finished, aye. Sure
haven't I just said five times?

Thomas Good-oh.

Thomas *smashes* **Mairtin** *twice across the head with the mallet,*
Mairtin *collapsing to the floor.*

Mary Thomas!

Mick *forcibly restrains* **Thomas** *from hitting* **Mairtin** *any more.*

Mick Leave him, Thomas, Christ! Thomas!

Mairtin (*dazed*)   What did he do that fer?

Thomas *stares at* **Mick** *blankly a while, sucking a second on his inhaler,* **Mick** *still holding him by the arms.*

Thomas   I think ... I think ... I think they're never going to promote me.

Mick *lets* **Thomas** *go.* **Mairtin** *has crawled onto a chair. In a blank daze,* **Thomas** *caresses* **Mairtin**'s *cheek, then gently touches his bloody head.*

Mairtin (*quietly, worried*)   Are you all right there, Tom?

Thomas *nods blankly.*

Thomas   I'll get you for all this someday, Mick Dowd. On me own soul I swear it.

Mick   Good luck so.

Thomas *nods, glances at the skull and at* **Mick**, *then exits.* **Mick** *sits with his wife's skull in his hands.* **Mary** *dabs at* **Mairtin**'s *bloody head with a hanky,* **Mairtin** *yelping slightly in pain.*

Mairtin   Ar Gran, ya bitch!

Mary *tuts.*

Mairtin   Ar Gran ya eejit, I meant. There'd better be none of your mouldy oul snot on that hanky now, Gran.

Mary   There's not, Mairtin. This is just me hanky for show.

Mairtin   Your hanky for show? Uh-huh?

He gives **Mick** *a look as if* **Mary** *is mad.*

D'ya hear this one?

Mick   I think maybe to hospital you should be going for yourself, now, Mairtin. A bang on the head can be awful serious if not looked at.

Mairtin   Ar hospitals are for poofs, sure.

Mick Hospitals aren't for poofs. They let anybody in.

Mairtin For poofs and for lesbos who can't take a middling dig.

Mary *tuts.*

Mairtin Wha? 'Lesbos' isn't swearing.

Mary Is it not?

Mairtin No. It's short for lesbians, y'know.

Mary Oh.

Mairtin 'Lesbos'. Y'know, like Mona McGhee in me school with the beard. (*Pause.*) Five times I've asked that bitch out and she still won't go.

Mick There's nothing the matter with lesbians, Mairtin. They're not doing harm to anybody.

Mairtin They're not, I suppose. And they're great at tennis. Em, you can leave me now, Gran. You're sort of getting on me nerves now, so you are.

Mary *stops attending to* **Mairtin** *and watches* **Mick** *with skull a while.*

Mairtin I suppose that'd be your missus, would it, Mick?

Mick It would.

Mairtin Uh-huh. Has she changed much since last you saw her?

Mick (*pause*) She has, Mairtin.

Mairtin Oh aye, it's been seven years, I suppose.

Mary (*pause*) Do you like bumpy slides, Mairtin?

Mairtin Bumpy slides? Where the hell did bumpy bloody slides come from?

Mary I won two goes on the bumpy slides at Leisureland if you'd want to go.

Mairtin You won't catch me going on the bumpy slides

with you, missus. I'd look a pure fool.

Mary   No, you could bring somebody else, I'm saying.

She gives **Mairtin** *the tickets.*

Mairtin   Oh. Aye. Thank you, Gran. Maybe Mona'd want to go. Heh, this has been a great oul day, this has. Drinking and driving and bumpy slides, and that oul battering them skulls to skitter was the best part of the whole day.

Mary *stares at* **Mick** *sternly.*

Mairtin   Would you need any help in giving your Oona a batter, Mick, or will you be handling that one yourself, now.

Mick   I'll be handling this one meself, Mairtin.

Mairtin   Good-oh.

Mick   And I'll be sending you a bill for the damage to me Anglia before the week's out.

Mairtin   Ar that's not fair, Mick.

Mick   Well life's not fair, Mairtin.

Mairtin (*confused slightly*)   It *is* fair. I like it anyways.

He gets to his feet and is overcome with dizziness. He sways around the room on weak legs and only manages not to collapse by clinging onto a wall.

Em, I think I might pop into that hospital after all. A biteen dizzy I am. I'll be seeing ye.

Mick   Be seeing you, Mairtin.

Mairtin (*pause*)   Be seeing you, Gran, I said!

Mary   Be seeing you, Mairtin.

Mairtin   Jeez, *deaf.*

Mairtin *takes a deep breath then staggers across the room, swaying, just making it out through the door, which he pulls behind him.*

Mary   So you do hammer the bones to skitter so.

Mick   Tonight was the first time ever that hammering happened, Maryjohnny, and only because wasn't I pure upset at Oona going missing on me . . .

Mary   And you expect me to believe you, the lies you never stop spouting?

Mick   What lies?

Mary   A fool could see Mairtin's injuries were no accident.

Mick   And, sure, didn't I admit that one outright, and sign a confession to the fact? How was that a lie?

Mary   And the lies o'er your poor Oona's dying then.

Mick   Oh you're still not going on about that fecking one, are ya? I have never lied o'er Oona dying. Never once.

Mary   Oh no? I must've been mistaken what I saw that night so, as along the two of ye drove.

Mick   What did you see? There was nothing to see.

Mary   Oh I suppose there was nothing to see, now.

Mick   If you've something to say to me, go ahead and say it outright and stop beating around the bush like a petrified fecking lummox. If you had seen anything made you think I'd killed Oona deliberate, why so would you've still come visiting me every night for the past seven year?

Mary   You had it right earlier.

Mary *finishes off her poteen with a flourish and puts the glass down.*

Mick   Oh, just to cadge me fecking booze, was it? Well be off on the road for yourself if that's the only reason you come here, with your hour-long weather bulletins and your Eamonn fecking Andrews spouting then. I never laid a finger on Oona, not from the day we married to the day she died, and if it's that you think you can upset me saying you saw something that night when there was nothing to see, then you've got another fecking think coming, girlie.

Mary   I'm saying nothing. Nothing at all am I saying. All I'm saying is you'll be meeting up with Oona again someday, Mick Dowd, and not just the bare skull but the spirit of her, and when you meet may down to the stinking fires of Hell she drag the rotten murdering bones of you, and may downhill from there for you it go. Goodbye to you now.

Mary *moves to the door.*

Mick   Maryjohnny?

Mary *turns.*

Mick   You've forgotten your flourescent pens, there.

She picks the pens up.

Mary   Thank you.

Mary *goes to the door again.*

Mick   And Maryjohnny? (*Pause.*) I didn't touch her. I swear it.

Mary *stares at him a moment, then exits.* **Mick** *looks at the rose locket then picks up the skull and stares at it a while, feeling the forehead crack. He rubs the skull against his cheek, trying to remember.*

Mick (*quietly*)   I swear it.

He caresses the skull again, kisses the cranium gently, and slowly exits to his room with it, still trying to remember. Lights fade to black as he goes.